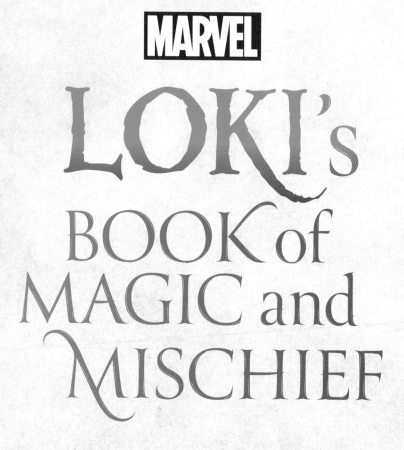

MARVEL

LOKI's BOOK of MAGIC and MISCHIEF

Tricks and Deceptions from the Prince of Illusions

Discovered, Translated, Edited, Annotated, and Tested by Robb Pearlman

Illuminated by Megan Levens

Smart Pop Books
An Imprint of BenBella Books, Inc.
Dallas, TX

T0015356

© 2023 MARVEL

Smart Pop is an imprint of BenBella Books, Inc.
10440 N. Central Expressway
Suite 800
Dallas, TX 75231
smartpopbooks.com | benbellabooks.com
Send feedback to feedback@benbellabooks.com

BenBella and *Smart Pop* are federally registered trademarks.

Printed in the United States of America
10 9 8 7 6 5 4 3 2 1

Library of Congress Control Number: 2023001382
ISBN 9781637741627 (print)
ISBN 9781637741634 (ebook)

Trick illustrations by Megan Levens
Magic consultant: Joe Fairchild
Editing by Elizabeth Smith
Copyediting by Lydia Choi
Proofreading by Michael Fedison and Isabelle Rubio
Text design and composition by Kit Sweeney
Cover design by Brigid Pearson
Printed by Versa Press

MARVEL PUBLISHING
Jeff Youngquist, VP, Production and Special Projects
Sarah Singer, Editor, Special Projects
Jeremy West, Manager, Licensed Publishing
Sven Larsen, VP, Licensed Publishing
David Gabriel, SVP Print, Sales & Marketing
C.B. Cebulski, Editor in Chief

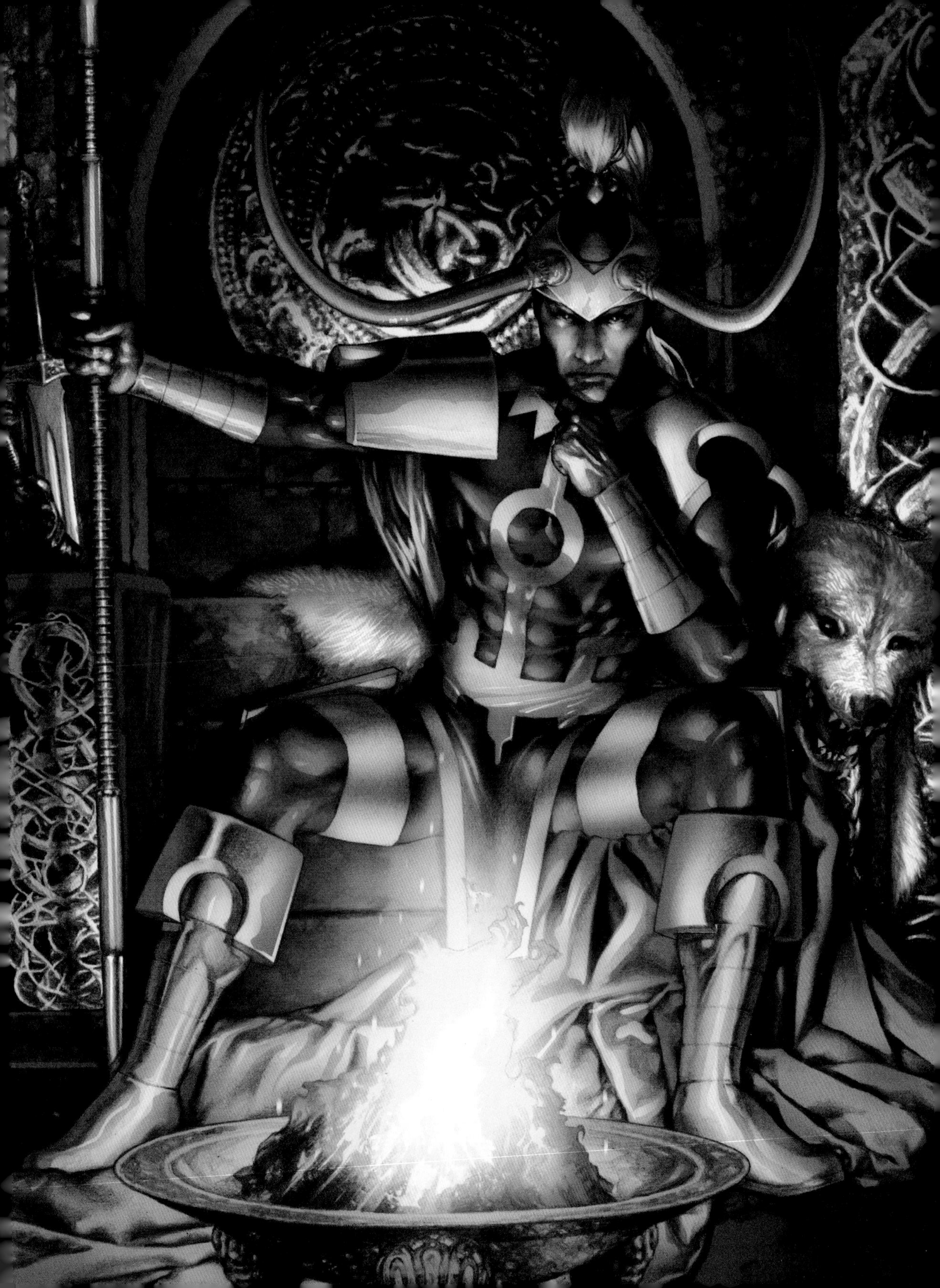

Dear Reader,

I've dedicated my life to rescuing and restoring ancient books that might otherwise have been lost to history. I have worked with teams of historians, archeologists, adventurers, scientists, and translators over the years, but I have decided that on this project I must work alone. It is too dangerous. I found a manuscript hidden deep within a cave covered in nearly impenetrable ice and ancient runes that warn of danger and mayhem—and if it is what I think it is, I have uncovered a thing far beyond our realm, and our realm of understanding. I cannot put the safety of my friends and teammates at risk as I uncover the secrets hidden in *Loki's Book of Magic and Mischief*.

Yes, *the* Loki. Trickster, brother of Thor, Prince of Asgard, God of Mischief himself. The first page of this codex, which appears to be written in Loki's own hand, begins with a welcome . . . and a warning. If I'm reading it correctly (and I know I am, thanks to my decades of studying Norse languages, ancient symbology, and alien cultures, my internship at Stark Industries, and my membership into many Asgard fan sites), Loki created this book for a potential future self to find in case he ever lost—and needed to relearn—his magical powers. As a noted expert and peer-reviewed professional, I am bound by solemn duty and pinky promises to avoid altering any artifact in my possession. My motto has always been "fidelity, precision, integrity," or, as it is in the original Latin, *fidelitas, praecisio, integritas*. (Or "idelityfay, eciscionpray, egrityintay" in the original Pig Latin.) So, in an effort to alter neither the text nor Loki's intention, this entire book, save this introduction and the notes I've added for organizational purposes, will read as if Loki is speaking directly to himself.

Which brings me to the warning: Loki states that this book is not for anyone else's eyes, let alone those of a Midgardian. Because of the looming threat, as compelled as I am to share this information with my fellow Midgardians, I am equally committed to shielding them from harm. Therefore, I feel duty-bound to test the spells and enchantments contained within the book, to perform them for myself. Given Loki's scrupulous instructions, I trust I—and then you—will soon be able to duplicate, if not master, his magic. ⟁

—Robb Pearlman

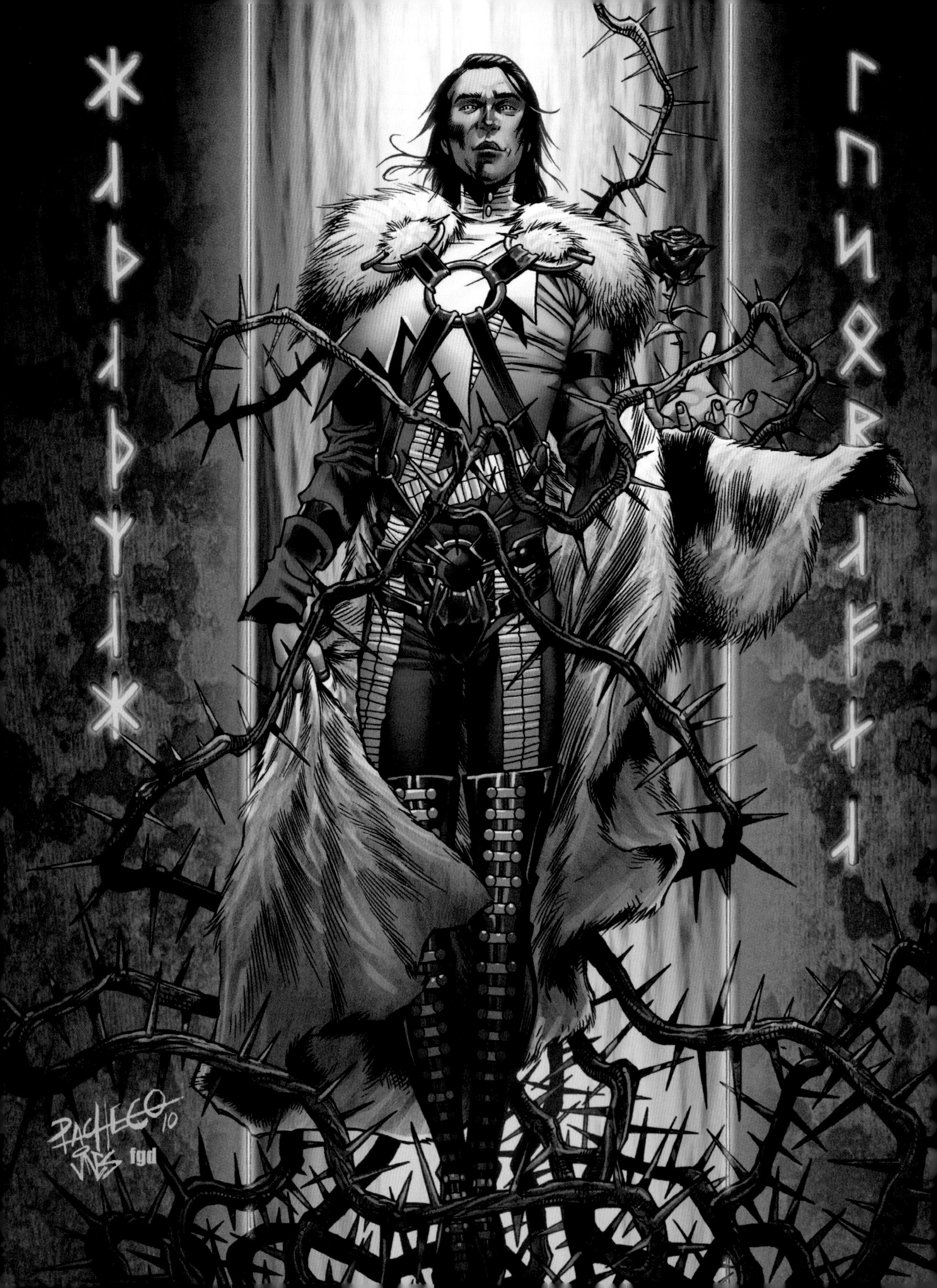
PACHECO 10
VINES fgd

Dear Loki,

If you are reading this, the day I have always known would come has, indeed, arrived. As sure as the ancient Asgardians foretold of Ragnarok, I knew that sometime, somehow, a skirmish with one or more of Earth's Mightiest Heroes would cause you to lose your magic and your memories. So, I created this book especially for you and hid it on Midgard in a place where you were once heralded as a god. A place you would be drawn to even if you lost all recollection of your life, your triumphs, and even the occasional setback. I knew you could, and would, find this because I know you. Better, as it happens, than you know yourself.

How? Because, Loki, *I am you*.

So, hold fast as these words—my words . . . *your* words—rekindle the magic and mischief buried within you. To build your confidence and experience, I have organized this book into three increasingly difficult parts. And, to spark your memories of conquests past, I have named these tricks after some of your most impressive moments and most notable foes, family, and sometime-friends. Turn the page to find out more . . .

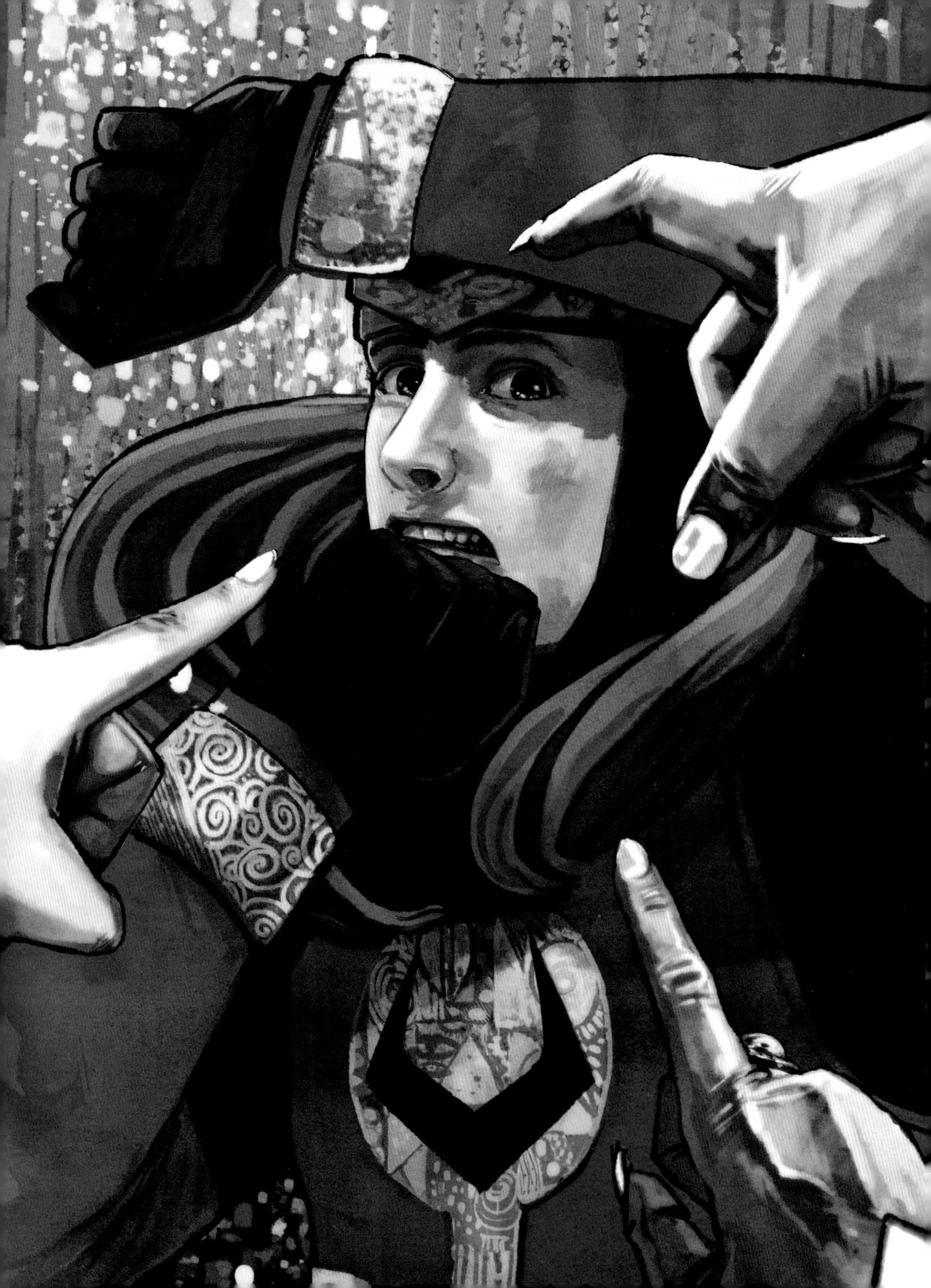

CONTENTS

PART 1

PART 2

PART 3

Note well, Loki: Before you can perform tricks that will surely astound and amaze anyone in the Ten Realms, you will need to arm yourself with the following:

banana

sturdy paper bowls

cardboard or sturdy paper

blanket or bedsheet

bucket or bowl

2 decks of playing cards
(at least 1 boxed)

clear plastic 2-liter bottle

handful of small,
multicolored candies

medium binder clips

opaque drinking vessel
(coffee mug or cup)

paper or plastic cup

fork

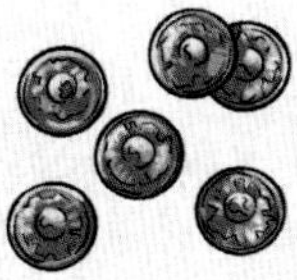

various Midgardian coins
(quarters and pennies)

white die
with black dots

glue

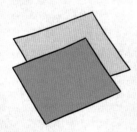

8½ x 11 inch construction
paper of different colors

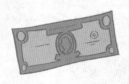

Midgardian paper
currency (dollar bill)

fabric glue

box of 6 crayons

clear glass drinking vessel

ice cubes

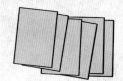

4 x 5 inch index cards

*11 x 17 inch pages of news-
paper or other thin paper*

ribbon

*lids of a medium
and large frying pan*

paper clips

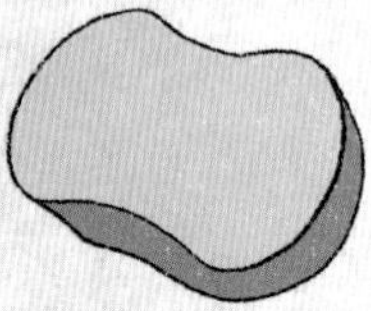

small sponge

lime

unsharpened pencils

*paper, plastic, or
lightweight straws*

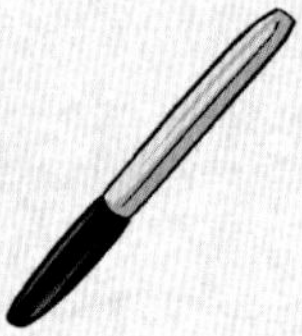

black marker

pieces of thin clear plastic

rubber bands

*cloth napkin, handkerchief,
or bandana*

sturdy paper plates

ruler

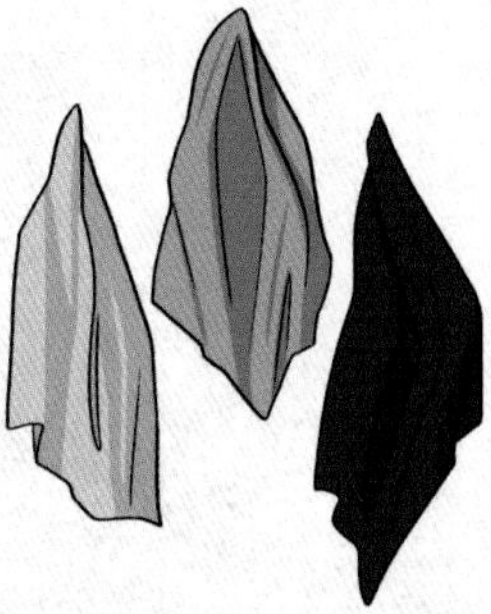

thin, lightweight scarves or handkerchiefs of the same size (preferably red, gold, and white)

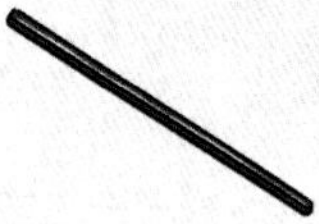

coffee stirrer

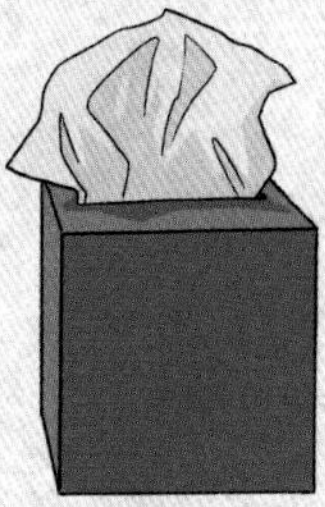

box of tissues

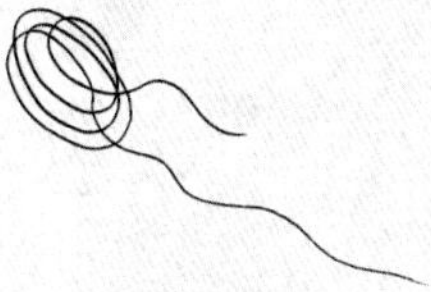

string

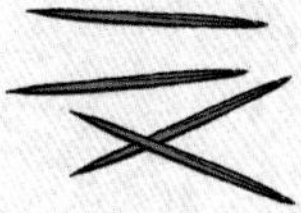

toothpicks

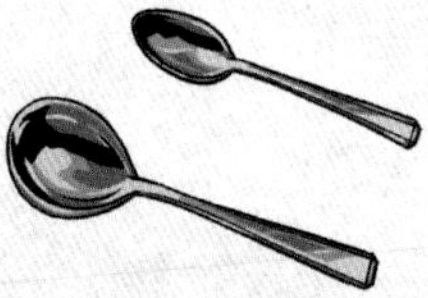

soupspoon and teaspoon

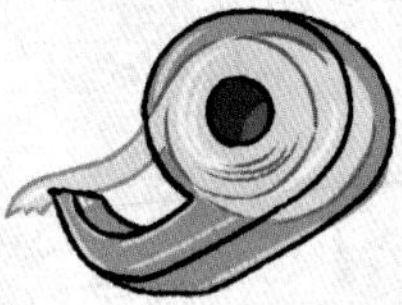

clear tape

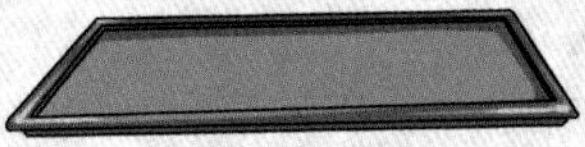

tray

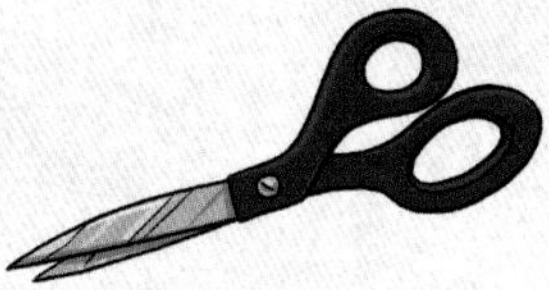

scissors

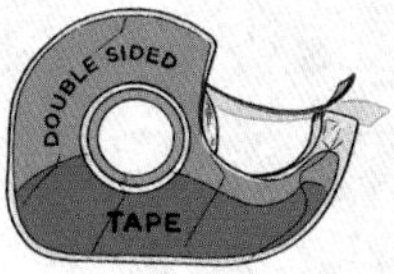
DOUBLE SIDED
TAPE

clear double-sided tape

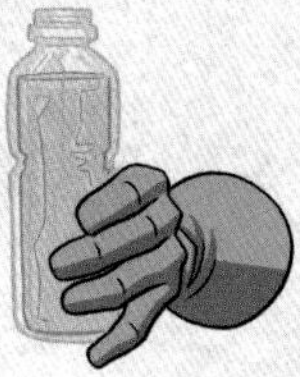

water

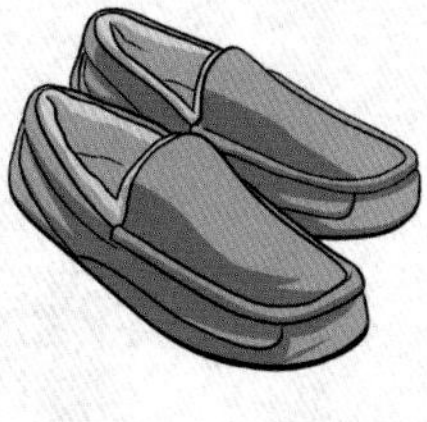

pair of lightweight slip-on shoes or slippers

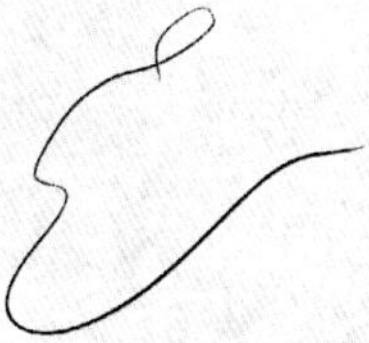

black thread

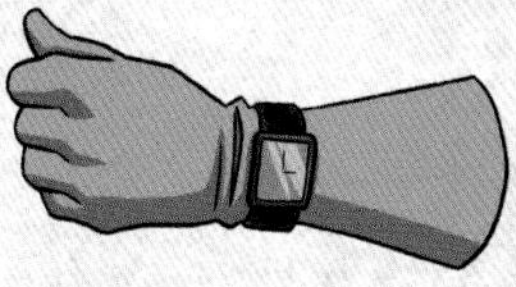

wristband, watch, Nega-Band, or bracelet

Last but not least, Loki, be warned: This book must be kept safely away out of the hands of any Frost Giant, human or mutant Midgardian, Dark Elf, Dísir, Kronan, or any other species. It offers a pathway to far more than magic. Once you unlock the secrets of this book, and the secrets locked within you, you will find yourself feeling rather . . . mischievous. One might even call it chaotic. Despotic? Righteous? Regardless, each lesson learned will surely spark something within you, growing ten-, twenty-, a hundredfold until you find yourself overflowing with untold remembrances of years of experience, unmatched power, and unbridled potential.

—LOKI—

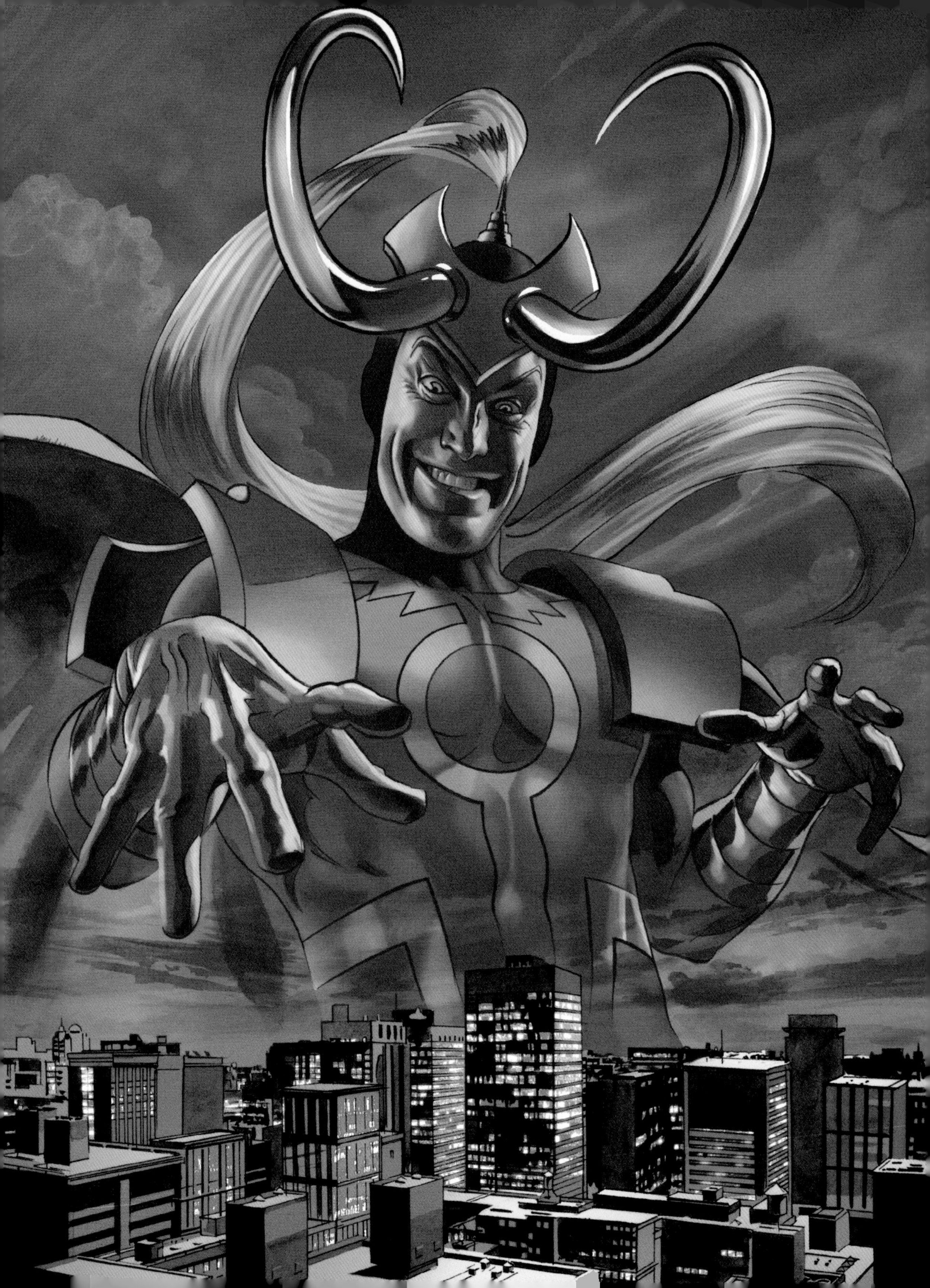

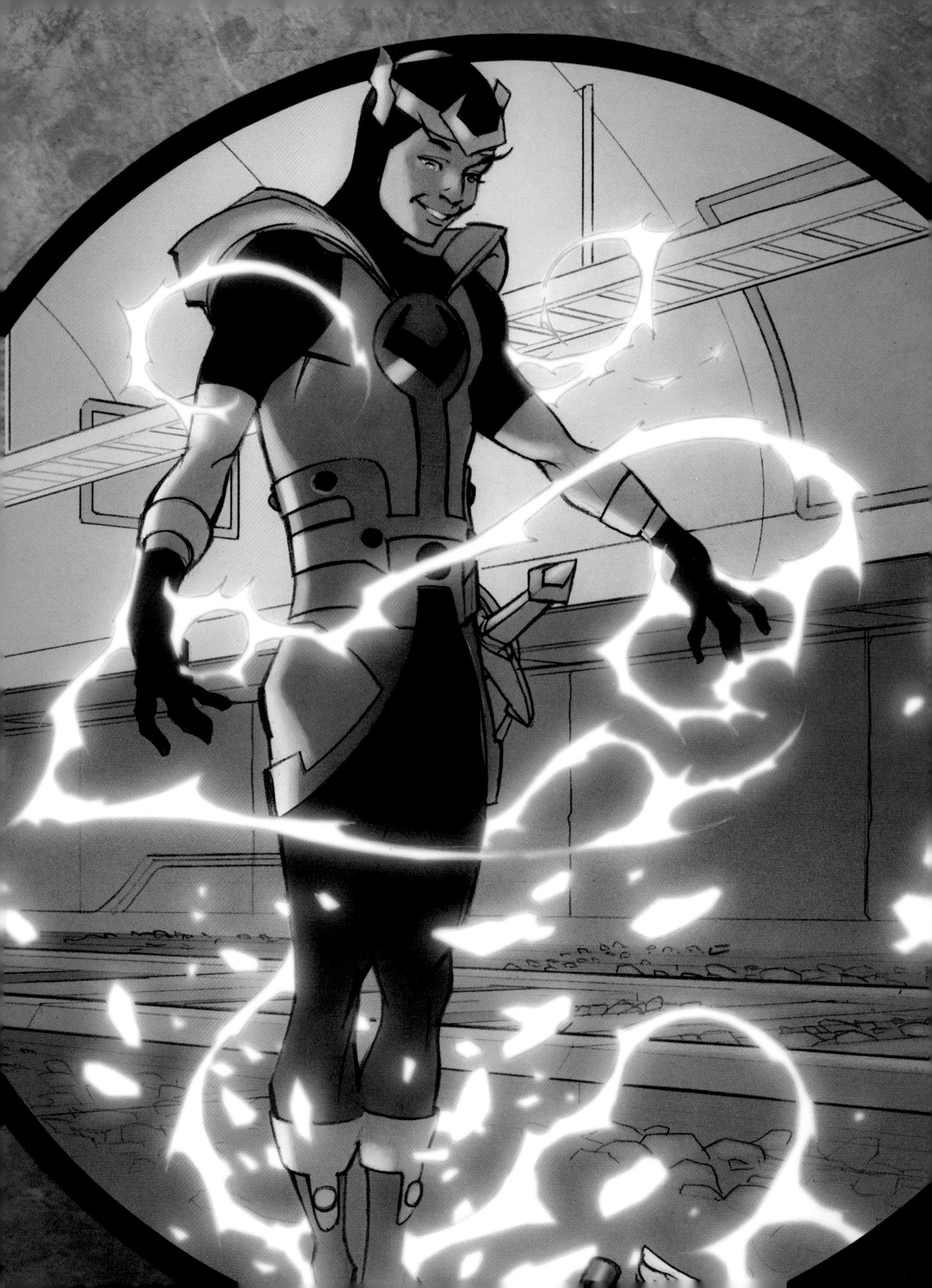

PART 1

The following tricks seem to be directed
toward a version of Loki who has little to
no experience wielding magic.

—RP

FILLINQ YOVR VAVLT

Midgardians value money. So much so that they will gladly help you enact your delightfully evil plans if you promise them a hefty payday. This trick not only shows them how you can magically double their wealth but will also guarantee their loyalty throughout the Ten Realms.

6 large Midgardian coins such as quarters

2 sturdy paper plates

1 small piece of cardboard or sturdy paper

clear tape or glue

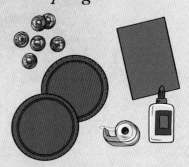

PREPARATION

Create a pocket by taping or gluing three edges of the cardboard or sturdy paper onto the bottom of one plate.

Fill the hidden pocket with three coins.

PERFORMANCE

1 Place the remaining three coins onto one of the plates.

Hold one plate in each hand. Place your thumb on top and your other fingers beneath to keep the coins from escaping the hidden pocket.

2 Gently tilt the plate with the coins so they slide off it and onto the other plate.

Continue tilting the plates and sliding the coins from one plate to the other. Distract your audience from seeing the hidden pocket by telling them just how much money they can earn by helping you plunder the multiversal treasures hoarded by S.H.I.E.L.D.

3 After a few moments, release your fingers just enough so the three hidden coins can slide out of the pocket and onto the plate with the other three coins.

Watch as the mortals marvel at how the number of coins is magically doubled.

Keep all six coins for yourself, and promise them coins and riches of their own.

Break that promise.

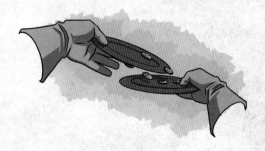

MS. NOT-SO-MARVELOUS

There are few things as entertaining as using the best assets of an opponent against them. This trick will remind you, and the audience, that your magic is powerful enough to wrap even the newest Avenger, Ms. Marvel, around your mischievous fingers.

MATERIALS NEEDED

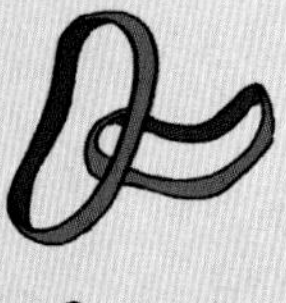

2 rubber bands. Make sure they are not a bright or easy-to-see color and that they fit snugly, but not too tightly, around your wrist (one too tight might wind up giving you a wrist burn that stings more than the wit of Ms. Marvel).

This trick might be more effective while performing wearing a long-sleeved shirt, a glove, or gauntlets, as the cuffs around your wrists will hide the rubber band.

PREPARATION

Place one rubber band around your left wrist and the other on the table.

PERFORMANCE

1 Pick up the rubber band and gently pull on it to show the audience it is as pliable, stretchy, and manageable as Kamala Khan.

Keep pulling on the rubber band, explaining that your arms are getting as tired as Kamala's youthful exuberance is tiresome. Say that you need a rest and lower your hands below the edge of the table where the audience cannot see.

2 Drop that rubber band and, as you bring your hands up again, hook the rubber band that has been around your left wrist with three fingers of your right hand and stretch it out.

3 Make a fist with your right hand so that end of the rubber band runs between your little finger and your ring finger, and your pointer finger and your thumb. Show only the front of your right fist to the audience.

4 As you continue to stretch the band, close your left hand so that side of the band runs between your little finger and your ring finger, and between your pointer finger and your thumb. Show only the front of your left fist to the audience.

As you continue to stretch the band, mimic punching your fists toward the audience, reminding them that no amount of stretching or punching from Ms. Marvel could be a match for your magic.

5 Let go of the rubber band. It will retract, snapping back onto your left wrist, but the audience will think it simply disappeared.

Open and wave your hands theatrically so the audience sees only your palms and outstretched fingers and not the rubber band around your wrist.

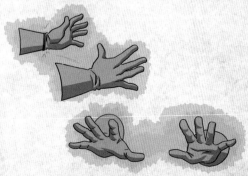

THE RISE OF LOKI

A deck of cards, like any noble court, is filled with courtiers all vying for fortune, favor, and (in your case) well-deserved power. But regardless of royal intrigue, public opinion, or galactic event, you—Loki, Prince of Asgard, Prince of Jotunheim, Prince of Lies—can and will rise above them all.

MATERIALS NEEDED

1 *deck of playing cards*

PREPARATION

Place the Ace of Diamonds at the top of the deck and the King of Clubs at the bottom.

PERFORMANCE

1 Hold the deck of cards vertically in your left hand, with the front of the cards facing toward the audience. (Your hand should also slightly block the cards.) Explain that the deck of cards represents some of your most memorable friends, enemies, and frenemies. Jane Foster, beloved of Thor, is the Queen of Hearts. Heimdall guarding the glittering Bifrost? The Jack of Diamonds. The formidable Sif, Runa, and Hildegarde? The Three of Spades. And that hammer-wielding cudgel of a brother, Thor? The King of Clubs.

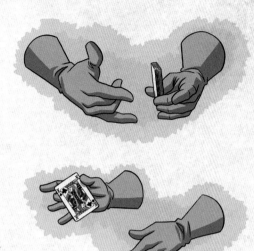

2 Now place the pointer finger of your right hand on the top of the deck.

Also extend your right pinky so it is touching the back of the last card in the deck, the Ace of Diamonds.

3 As you raise your pointer finger up, lightly push against the cards with your pinky. Lo, the Ace of Diamonds will rise, seemingly beckoned by your pointer finger. Remind the audience that no matter what realm, no matter what era, no matter what challenge, *you* are the bright shining future of Asgard and will rise, again and again.

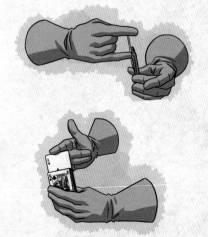

VARIANTS

You have undergone countless physical and sartorial transformations over your millennia of existence. But one thing never changes: you are and always will be unmistakably you—Loki, God of Mischief. This trick reminds your soon-to-be subjects that variations in your appearance can and do happen . . . and not just because of your shape-shifting prowess.

MATERIALS NEEDED

1 *large cloth napkin, handkerchief, or bandana*

1 *soupspoon*

1 *teaspoon*

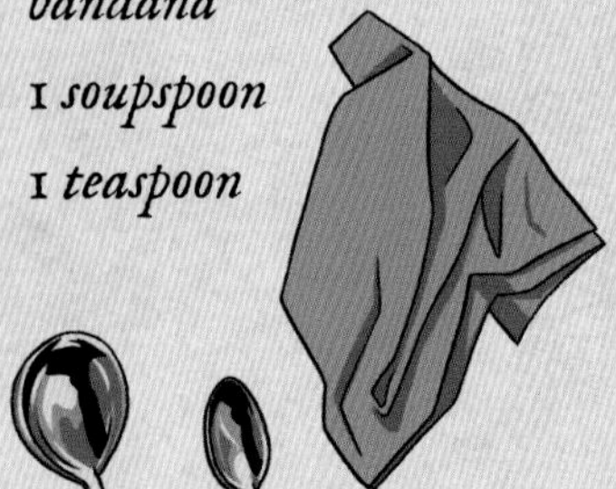

PREPARATION

Lay the napkin flat on the table so it forms a diamond, with the four corners pointing to your right, your left, toward you, and away from you.

Fold the napkin in half so it forms a triangle. The long base of the triangle should be closest to you, and the peak of the triangle will point away from you.

Place the teaspoon inside the folded napkin, about halfway between the right and left points.

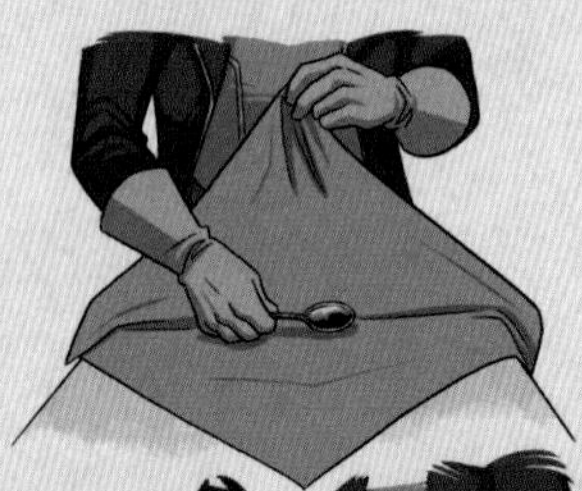

Fold in the corners of the napkin so it looks like what you would find on a table setting. Without disturbing the teaspoon inside the napkin, set it all to the side or beneath the table.

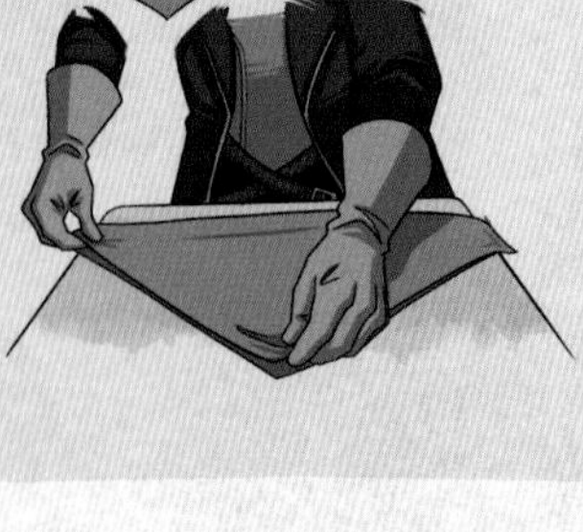

PERFORMANCE

1 Place the soupspoon and napkin on the table. Unfold the napkin just until the audience sees the large triangle (which is hiding the teaspoon).

Remind the audience that your shape-shifting abilities know no bounds. Place the soupspoon on top of the base of the folded napkin, near the teaspoon hidden underneath.

2 Explain that though your size or clothing may look different, your soul is never changing. Starting with the folded base of the napkin, roll the soupspoon up. When you see the two corners of the napkin flip over, stop rolling.

3 Grab each of these two corners and peel back just the top layer of the napkin. This will turn the napkin inside out and expose the teaspoon (and hide the soupspoon). Remind the audience that whether you are a giant among Midgardians or a runt among Frost Giants . . . You. Are. Loki.

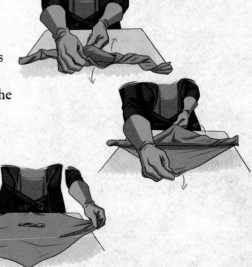

THE BALANCE OF POWER

You know (better than most) that the only thing more difficult than obtaining power is maintaining it. You must constantly balance your attentions toward fending off your enemies, heroes, and—in your case—your family. This balancing trick will prove to any naysayers just how well suited you are to lead.

MATERIALS NEEDED

2 playing cards (one should be a King of any suit)

scissors

clear tape

1 paper or plastic drinking vessel

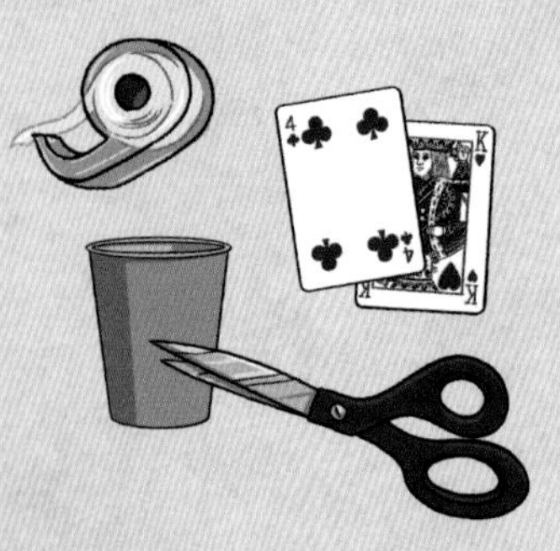

PREPARATION

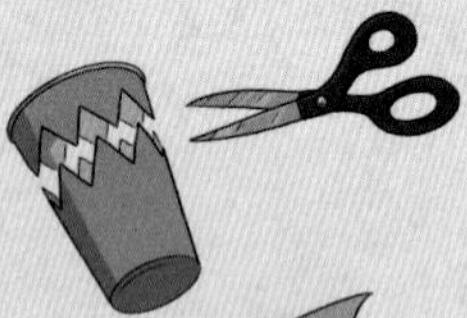

Cut a diagonal pattern into the top of the drinking vessel so the vessel resembles a crown.

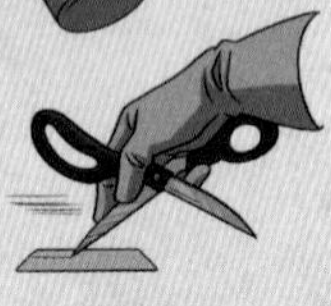

Cut one card (not the King) in half vertically.

Line up one of the halves over the back of the King card. The designs on the back of the half card should precisely match the back of the King card.

Tape the half card to the King card along one vertical edge. This will make a hinge for the half card to swing out, as well as create a tripod that allows the King card to stand up on its own.

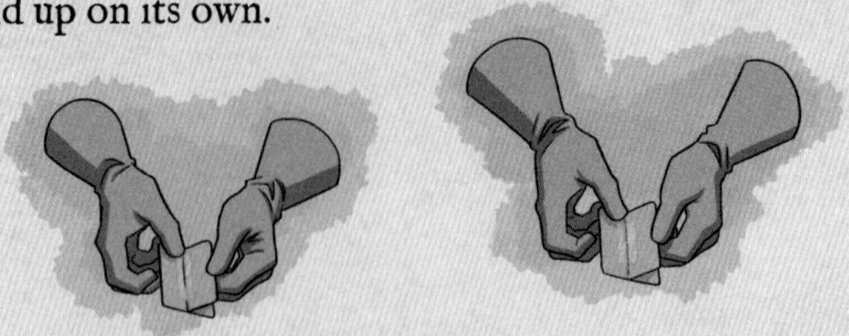

PERFORMANCE

1 Use your right hand to hold up the King card so the audience can see its face. Turn your hand so they can see the back of the card, then quickly show its face again. Then hold the card on the table so it rests on its bottom edge.

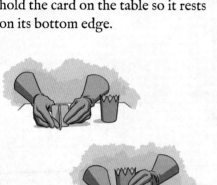

2 Compare being a king and the precarious nature of power to a playing card standing up on its own. As you speak, use your right thumb to gently swing the hinge out ninety degrees. Seen only by you, the top edges of the cards will form a "T." This will allow the card to stand on its own.

3 However, continue to make a show of keeping the card upright on the table with your right hand. With your left hand, set the "crown" drinking vessel on the top edges of the "T" formed by the hinge.

4 Take your time to balance the drinking vessel on the card. Distract the audience by explaining that though you are perfectly suited to any throne, you find ruling Midgard to be particularly appealing. Move both hands away with a dramatic flourish, and the vessel will appear to stand on top of the card, proving your worth.

STEALING TREASURE

Some Midgardians believe that money is the root of all evil. I am not sure that is entirely true, but money does come in handy when you are trying to incentivize mortals to assist in your schemes. And because no bank or credit union will offer you a line of credit—or even an ATM card—and you no longer have access to the overflowing coffers that Odin hoards for himself, you will have to get . . . creative . . . in how you secure funding.

MATERIALS NEEDED

2 pieces of construction paper that are the same color

1 clear plastic or glass drinking vessel

1 pencil

scissors

glue

1 Midgardian coin

1 large cloth napkin, handkerchief, or bandana

1 tray

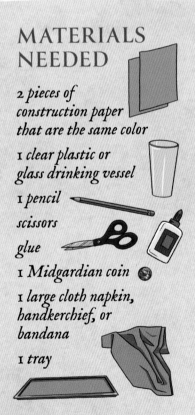

PREPARATION

Place the drinking vessel upside down on one piece of construction paper. Trace around the opening of the drinking vessel until you have a circle exactly the same size as the opening.

Cut the circle out, glue it over the mouth of the glass, and let that dry. Then trim off any excess paper or rough edges.

Place the other piece of construction paper on a tray. Set the drinking vessel upside down on that paper. The glued-on paper covering the mouth of the drinking vessel should blend into the construction paper.

PERFORMANCE

1 Place the tray with the upside-down glass on the paper upon a tabletop.

Place the coin onto the construction paper, not too far away from the drinking vessel. Explain to the audience the plight of having a grand scheme but no way to pay for it.

Cover the drinking vessel with the cloth.

2 Move the drinking vessel smoothly over the coin. It should appear to the audience as if you are not lifting the drinking vessel at all. Remind them that you are Loki and have more schemes than there are coins in the realm.

3 Remove the cloth to reveal that the coin has disappeared from their dimension and into your own vaults.

But, because you are generous, cover up the drinking vessel again with the cloth.

Move the drinking vessel smoothly away from (and off of) the coin.

Remove the cloth. The coin has reappeared, proving that you will only take what is necessary. And what is rightfully yours.

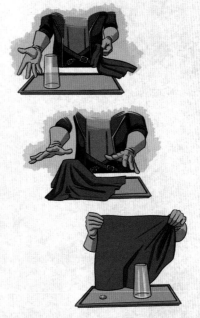

THE ARROW OF HAWKEYE

You have battled gods, monsters, and Avengers wielding enormous powers. So the threat posed by one man with a bow and arrow is laughable. This feat demonstrates just how easily your magic can defeat any arsenal of trick arrows the archer may have.

MATERIALS NEEDED

1 *clear glass drinking vessel*

water

1 *blank 4 x 5 inch index card*

1 *black marker*

ruler

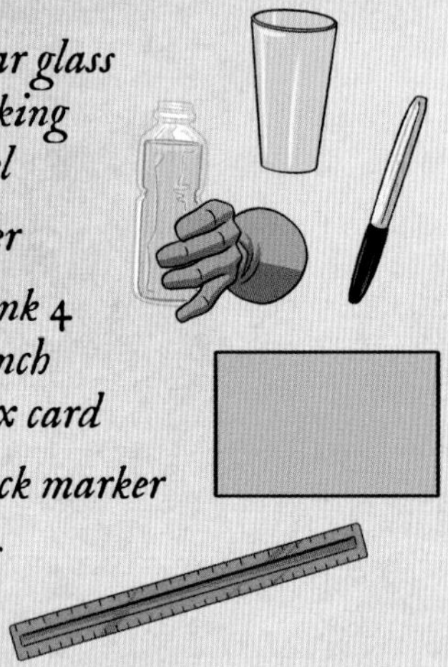

PREPARATION

Measure the opening of the drinking vessel. Draw an arrow the same length as the opening in the middle of the index card.

Fill the drinking vessel about ¾ full with water.

PERFORMANCE

1 Hold the card above the glass so the audience clearly sees the arrow pointing to their right (your left).

2 As you slowly lower the card behind the drinking vessel, the water and glass will refract the image so it looks to the audience that the arrow reverses direction and points to their left (your right). Explain that though the arrows of Clint Barton may shoot straight, your skills as a magician can deflect his airborne weapons—and turn them back on him.

3 Slowly raise the card above the glass, demonstrating that you—not he—have ultimate control over his arsenal, then lower it one more time so it looks as if it is, once again, pointing to their left.

DEFEATING THE AVENGERS

You never get credit for the good things you do. (Even if you do them accidentally.) It is very frustrating! Most people forget—or want to forget—that you were the reason Earth's Mightiest Heroes came together in the first place. This is the perfect trick to remind everyone just how important you are.

MATERIALS NEEDED

2 sturdy paper bowls

5 Midgardian coins (three large and two small)

Clear double-sided tape

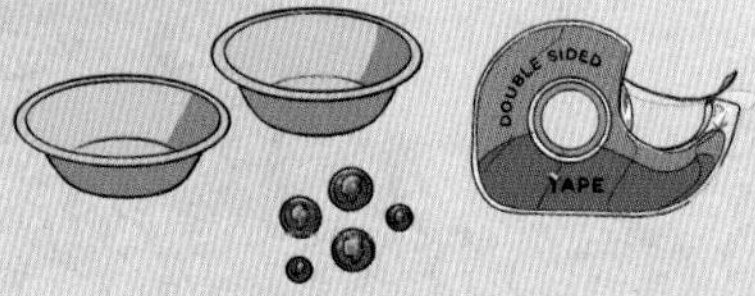
DOUBLE SIDED
TAPE

PREPARATION

Stick three small pieces of double-sided tape in one of the bowls.

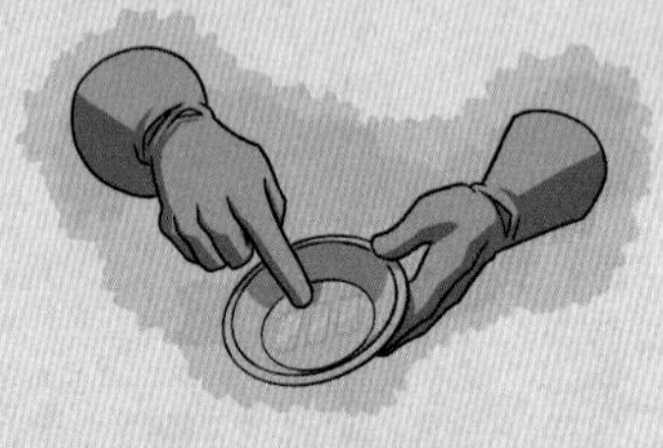

Place the coins into the other bowl.

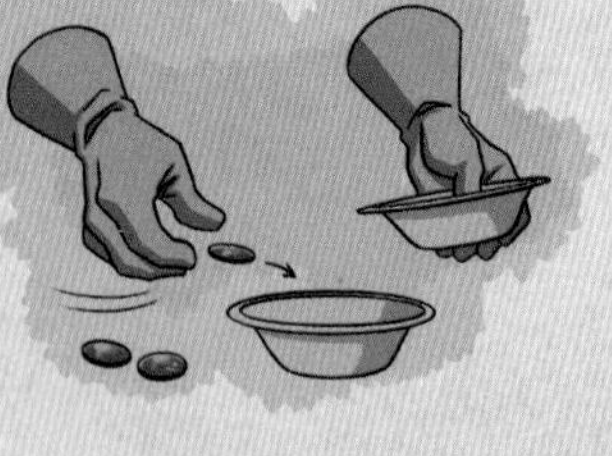

PERFORMANCE

1 Remind the audience that, if it were not for you, the Avengers would never have formed. Quickly hold up the bowls so the audience sees that one holds the coins and the other looks empty.

2 Say the names of each of the founding members of the team. Pick up one large coin, representing Thor. Place it, firmly, inside the other bowl and directly on top of one of the pieces of double-sided tape. Do the same for a large coin representing Iron Man and another large coin representing the Hulk. Now pick up the remaining two small coins, representing Ant-Man and the Wasp, and toss them on top of the three coins.

3 Show the audience all five coins in the bowl. Rattle them around as a reminder of how you drove them crazy in battle!

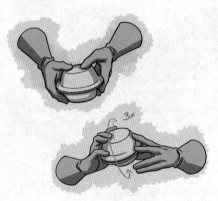

4 Turn the empty bowl upside down and place it on top of the bowl with coins.

Remind the audience that no amount of gamma radiation, human ingenuity, or Asgardian worthiness is a match for your cunning. Grip the edges of the bowls together so the two coins do not escape and flip them over three times. (The bowl with the coins stuck to it should now be on top, with the two small coins in the bottom bowl.)

5 Move the top bowl to the side—still upside down—and reveal only the two small coins left in the bottom bowl, proving that you could easily take out heavy hitters the Hulk, Iron Man, and Thor. (Earth's Mightiest Heroes? More like Zeros.) Spill the remaining two small coins out onto the table. Pick them up and drop them dismissively to the floor—as you would do (and have done) to Ant-Man and the Wasp.

TOO MANY LOKIS

Any universe is better with a Loki in it. But there is nothing better (or sometimes worse) than when Lokis from various universes join forces.

MATERIALS NEEDED

Midgardian paper currency (dollar bill)
2 paper clips

PERFORMANCE

1 Hold the bill, representing the known universe, up to the audience. Ask them if they know what an Einstein-Rosen Bridge is. (*Note: they will not know.*)

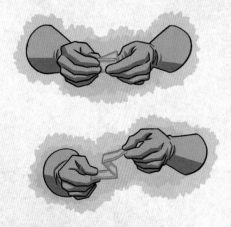

2 Explain the theory to them as condescendingly as possible: a black hole can serve as a connection between two locations in space—or the same location but in different universes. Represent that by folding the bill in thirds so its shape resembles what they recognize as a "Z," with the front layer facing the audience (the top of the "Z"), the back layer facing you (the bottom of the "Z"), and the middle layer between them (the slanted part of the "Z"). About ⅜ of an inch of the front layer and the back layer should stick out so you can hold the bill on either side with your fingers.

3 Entities can use Einstein-Rosen Bridges to traverse points in space or universes. At the top right edge of the folded bill, at the crease, clip the first paper clip to the front layer and the middle layer. This represents you, the Loki that stands before the audience.

4 On the top left edge of the folded bill, at the crease, clip the second paper clip to the back layer and the middle layer. This represents a Loki from another universe.

5 Grip the edge of the front layer of the bill with your right hand and the edge of the back layer of the bill with your left hand.

Simultaneously and quickly pull the bill right and left.

6 The paper clips will jump off the bill yet be mysteriously linked together. Explain that this represents the chaos that can happen if two versions of the same person from different universes join together. And proof that it is better—especially for them—that you work alone.

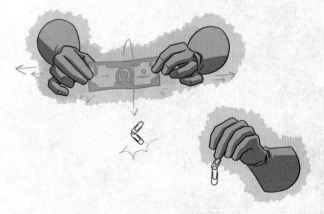

LOKI OF ASGARD

People of all realms need to be reminded that you would never be so foolish as to become an easy target. Your powers of illusion will keep you from harm by forcing any foe—be they Asgardian or Midgardian—to disbelieve what their own eyes are showing them.

MATERIALS NEEDED

5 playing cards: Three of Spades, Three of Hearts, Three of Diamonds, Jack of Diamonds, and Ace of Clubs

glue

paper clip

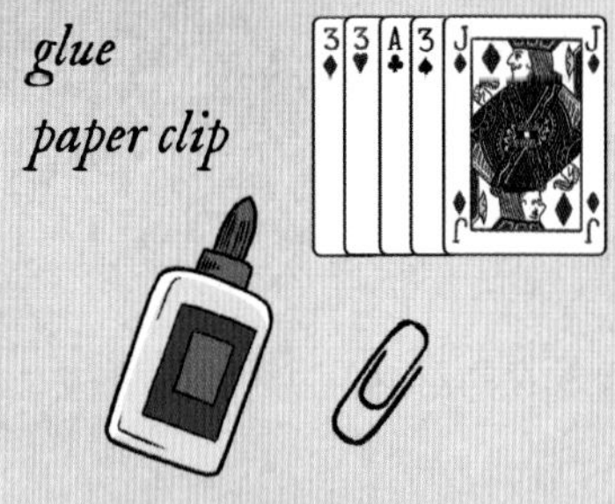

PREPARATION

Arrange the cards in a line so that the Ace of Clubs is in the middle.

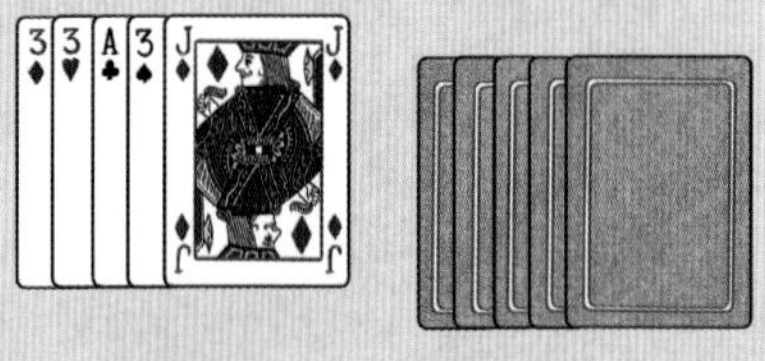

Overlap them so just the "3," "J," and "A" on the cards show.

Glue them together.

PERFORMANCE

1 Show the audience the five cards, representing five of the most powerful Asgardians, Lady Sif and the Warriors Three: Hogun, Volstagg, and Fandral—and, of course, you.

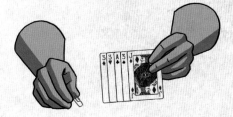

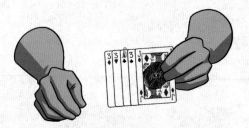

2 Invite an audience member to slip a paper clip over the card that stands out in the middle—the one with truly the most power—you. The Ace of Clubs.

Once they clip it, ask them, "Are you sure you clipped Loki, the Ace of Clubs?"

3 After they say yes (because they are gullible), turn the cards around to show the backs of the cards to the audience. The paper clip is now clipped to the card at the end.

4 Laugh at their silliness but let an audience member try it again.

5 It will be the same result, of course—the paper clip that they thought was clipped to you in the middle appears to be clipped to the end card. Why? Because you, Loki, would never allow anyone to stab you in the back.

THE HORNS OF YOUR HELMET

Midgardians love symbols. The Avengers would be nothing without their signature "A" slapped on everything from Helicarriers to lunch boxes. Black Widow would be just another spy without the iconic spider-like icon on her belt buckle. And the Hulk would be just another green buffoon without his . . . purple pants. You know the importance of presentation, and nothing gets people screaming like your famed horned helmet. This trick will keep them guessing, and screaming, for more.

MATERIALS NEEDED

2 pieces of 8½ x 11 inch construction paper of different colors, preferably green and yellow

1 lid of a large frying pan

1 lid of a medium frying pan

pencil

ruler

scissors

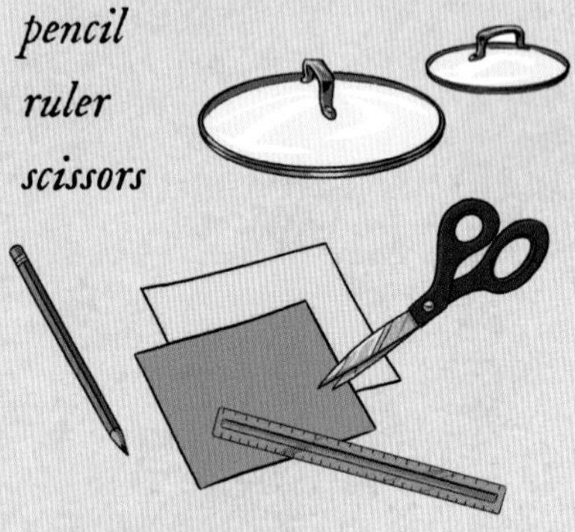

PREPARATION

Place the large frying-pan lid along the 8½ inch side of the paper. Use the pencil to draw a half circle along its top edge.

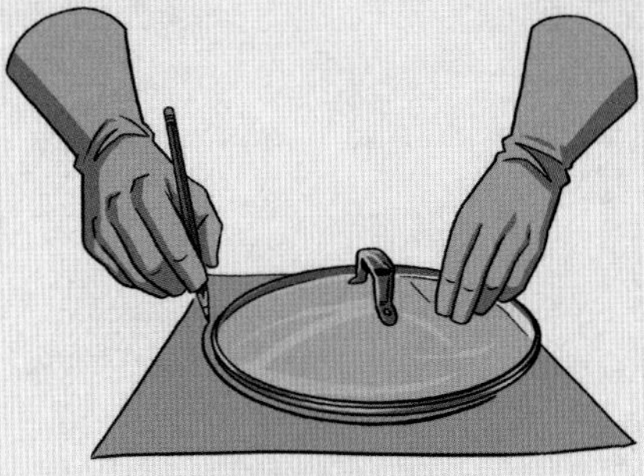

Place the medium frying-pan lid about two inches below the half circle you have just created. Use the pencil to draw a half circle along its top edge.

Use the ruler to draw a straight line to connect each side of the two half circles.

Place that paper on top of the other.

Use the scissors to cut out two identical shapes.

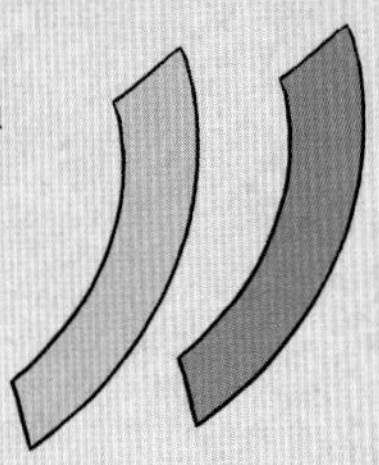

PERFORMANCE

1 Hold the shapes up to your forehead so they resemble the horns that protrude from your famed and feared helmet. Tell the audience to look at the two horns very carefully because there is something special about them—and not just because they are yours.

Then hold the green horn above the yellow one and ask which one is bigger.

Because of the optical illusion created, the audience members will be fooled into claiming that the yellow one is bigger.

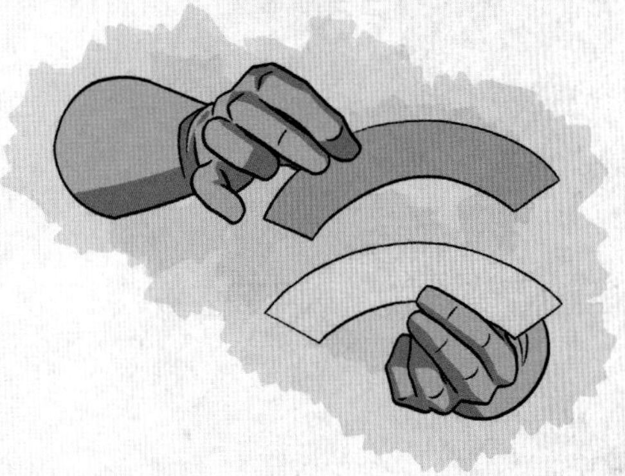

CONTINUED . . .

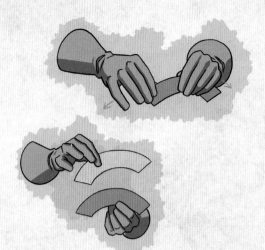

2 Put the horns down and use your fingers to pretend to stretch the green horn.

Hold them up again, this time with the yellow horn above the green one. Because they are simple Midgardians who actually believe what their eyes are showing them, the audience will now think that the green horn is bigger.

3 Offer to reverse the effect and pretend to stretch the yellow one.

Hold the horns up again, with the green horn above the yellow one. The audience will see that the yellow horn is again bigger.

4 Turn the two horns over and compare them edge to edge, with the arc of the yellow horn tucked under the arc of the green one, their edges touching. The yellow horn will look much bigger.

Mischievously snap your fingers and compare them again side by side, this time with the arc of the green horn tucked under the arc of the yellow horn, their edges touching. The green one will now look much bigger.

5 Now line them up on top of each other to show that they are, bafflingly to the Midgardians' paltry optical sense, the same size.

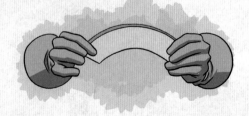

THE GOD OF STORIES

Some gods rely on only one or two stories that portray their worthiness. But not you. The many true—and not *entirely* true—tales you tell of magic, mischief, and heroics will surely be told by bards and scholars until Ragnarok. And maybe even beyond!

MATERIALS NEEDED

boxed deck of cards

scissors

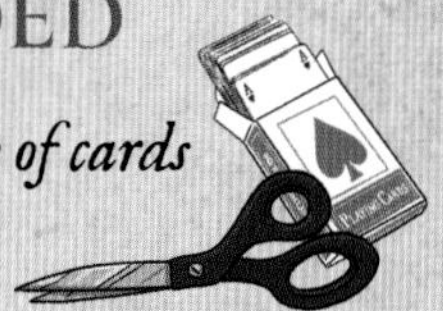

PREPARATION

Remove the cards from the box.

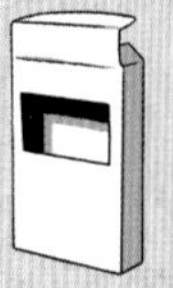

Use the scissors to cut a hole near the top of the back of the box, big enough for you to push your thumb into.

Replace the cards in the box.

PERFORMANCE

1 Hold the box of cards in your right hand with your four fingers at the front and your thumb inserted into the hole you cut into the back of the box.

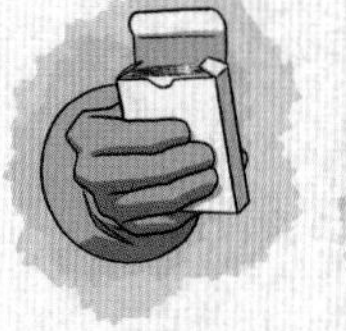

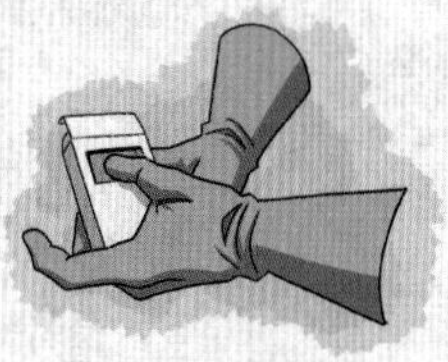

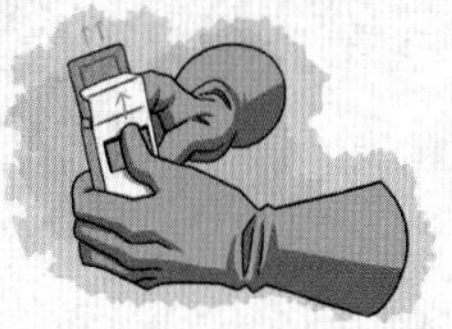

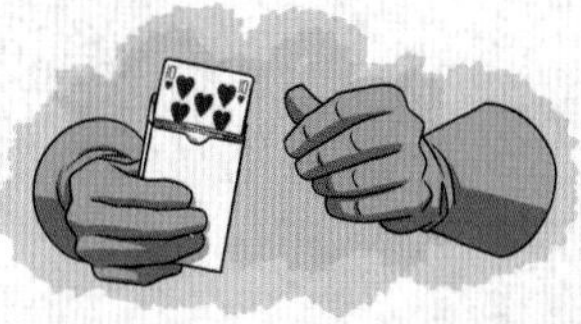

2 Pinch the box between your fingers and thumb, and gently push a card up with your thumb. To the audience, the card will seem to rise mysteriously out of the box.

3 As the card rises, take it from the box with your left hand. Toss the card into the audience, telling them about the first time you fought the Avengers.

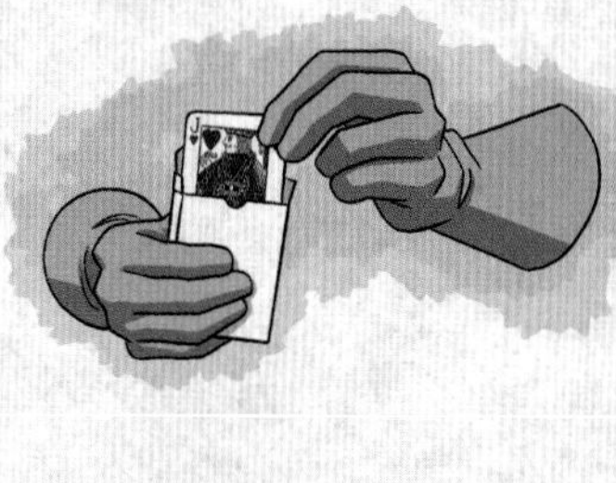

Continue pushing the cards up with your right thumb, taking them out with your left hand, tossing them into the audience, and regaling the audience with stories . . . and lies . . . until there are no cards left. Or you grow bored.

TAKE A BREAK

World domination can be an exhausting exercise. It is important for you to take the time and sit back on your throne to enjoy the spoils of war that you have worked, schemed, and plotted so hard for. This trick will reinforce to your subjects that while you may be taking a break—you are still in charge.

MATERIALS NEEDED

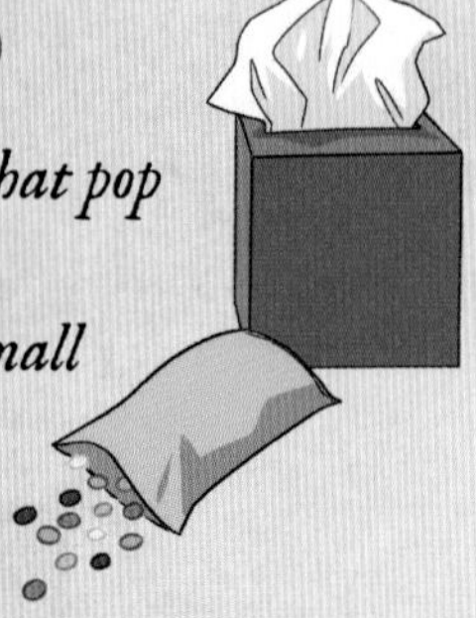

Box of tissues that pop up from the top

A handful of small multicolored candies

PREPARATION

Lay a tissue flat on the table.

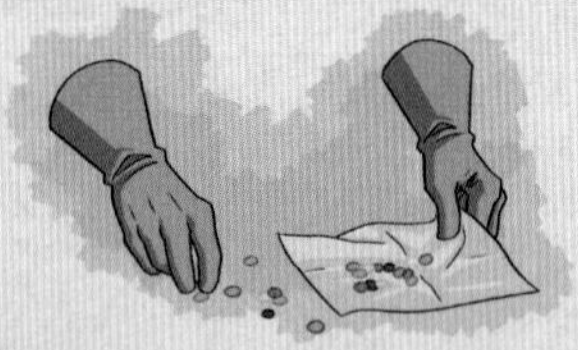

Place the candies in the center of the tissue.

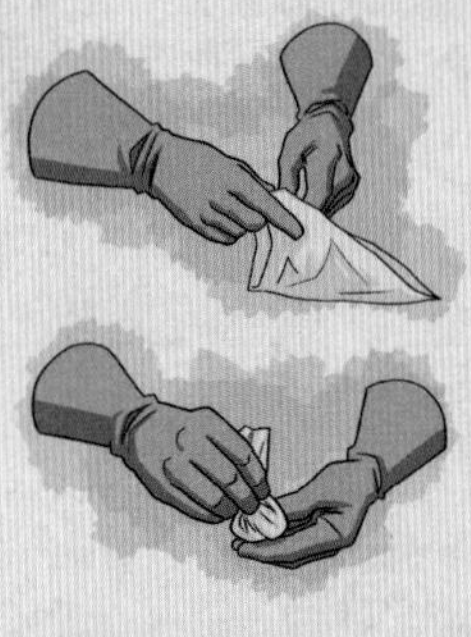

Fold the tissue around the candies and twist it at the top to close, securing the candies inside.

Place the tissue box off to the side near where you are performing. Place the tissue-wrapped candy behind the tissue that is extending out of the box so it is hidden from the audience.

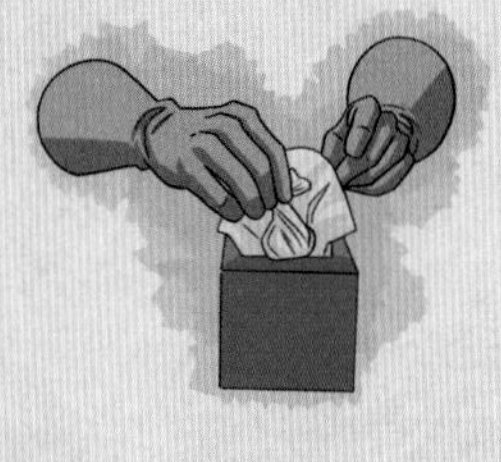

PERFORMANCE

1 Tell the audience even gods such as yourself require a rest. Ask for their patience as you reach for a tissue to wipe the perspiration from your brow. Approach or reach for the box of tissues.

2 Grab the tissue out of the box, along with the hidden pre-wrapped bag of candies.

Gently bunch the tissues into your hand as you pat your forehead. Tell the audience that you are hungry and will now manifest a snack for yourself.

3 Bring the tissues down to the table and tear open the tissues to reveal the candies. Keep them all for yourself.

WATCHING YOUR BACK

You have built quite a reputation for yourself. Unfortunately, after years of shifting alliances, that reputation may put you in jeopardy. This trick will remind you, and the audience, to always look out.

MATERIALS NEEDED

Midgardian paper currency (dollar bill)

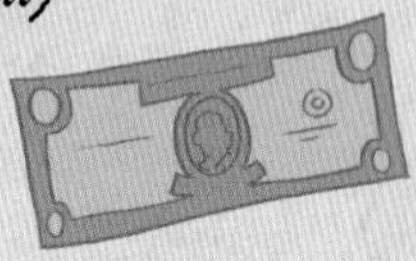

PERFORMANCE

1 Take this opportunity to regale the audience with tales of how you have shifted your allegiances from evil to not quite good to ... completely self-serving. Show the dollar bill to the audience, with the portrait of George Washington right-side up and facing the audience.

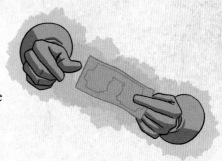

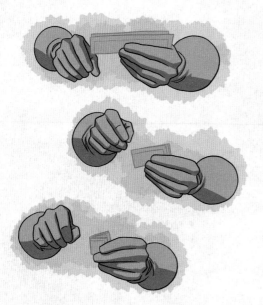

2 Fold the dollar bill in half, lengthwise, with the crease downward so the edges of the bill form a "V" shape, open to the top.

Fold the bill in half again, this time crosswise, so that the crease is on the right. The edges of the bill should form a "V" shape, open to the top.

Fold the bill in half again, again crosswise, so that the crease is on the right. The edges of the bill should form a "V" shape, open to the top.

3 Unfold the bill by grabbing the innermost layer and pulling out, which reverses the bill.

Unfold the rest of the bill and reveal that the portrait of George Washington is now upside down. A lesson to yourself, and the audience, that before setting on a course of action, you must always look left, right, up, and down.

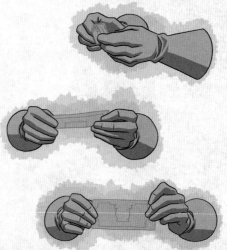

THE MAGIC WAND

Doctor Strange and Wong possess and protect many magic wands in their Sanctum Sanctorum. It is . . . adorable . . . that Strange, his allies, and even his enemies rely on trinkets such as the Wand of Xyggondo and the Wand of Watoomb to channel magical energy. This trick shows that you have no need of a wand—and that wands are, in fact, easily broken.

MATERIALS NEEDED

2 pencils

wristband, watch, bracelet, or Nega-Band

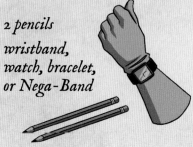

PREPARATION

Place the wristband on your left wrist.

Slide one pencil between the wristband and your wrist. One-third of it should extend as far as the palm of your outstretched left hand.

PERFORMANCE

1 Stand so your left side is facing the audience. Hold the other pencil vertically in your left fist, keeping the back of your hand toward the audience so they do not see the pencil tucked under your wristband.

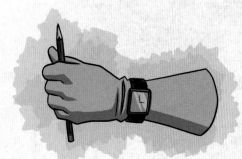

Keeping the back of your left hand facing the audience, grip your left wrist with your right hand. Extend your right index finger and use it to gently roll the vertical pencil between the pencil extending from your wristband and your left palm. When it is secure, your right hand and finger should also cover the hidden pencil.

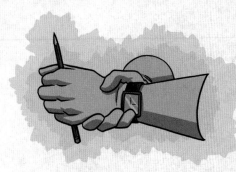

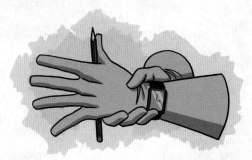

2 Open the fingers of your left hand, one by one, to show the audience how the pencil is floating in the air behind your hand.

CONTINUED . . .

3 Remind the audience that Doctor Strange is a cut-rate magician compared to you. There are always simple explanations for his silly tricks. To prove your point, turn so the audience can see the other side of your left arm with the pencil held vertically by your right index finger in your left palm. Make sure you do not move your right hand and show the hidden pencil, however.

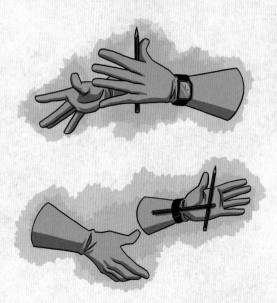

4 Say to the audience that you, Loki, will now prove you have no need for a wand and will repeat the trick. Turn so the audience only sees your left side again. But this time, open your right hand, releasing your left wrist. The audience will see that the pencil is floating in your left hand again—but your right hand is no longer supporting it.

Laugh as the audience gasps. Then pluck the floating pencil from midair with your right hand, showing that you are a far more supreme sorcerer than Strange or Wong could ever be.

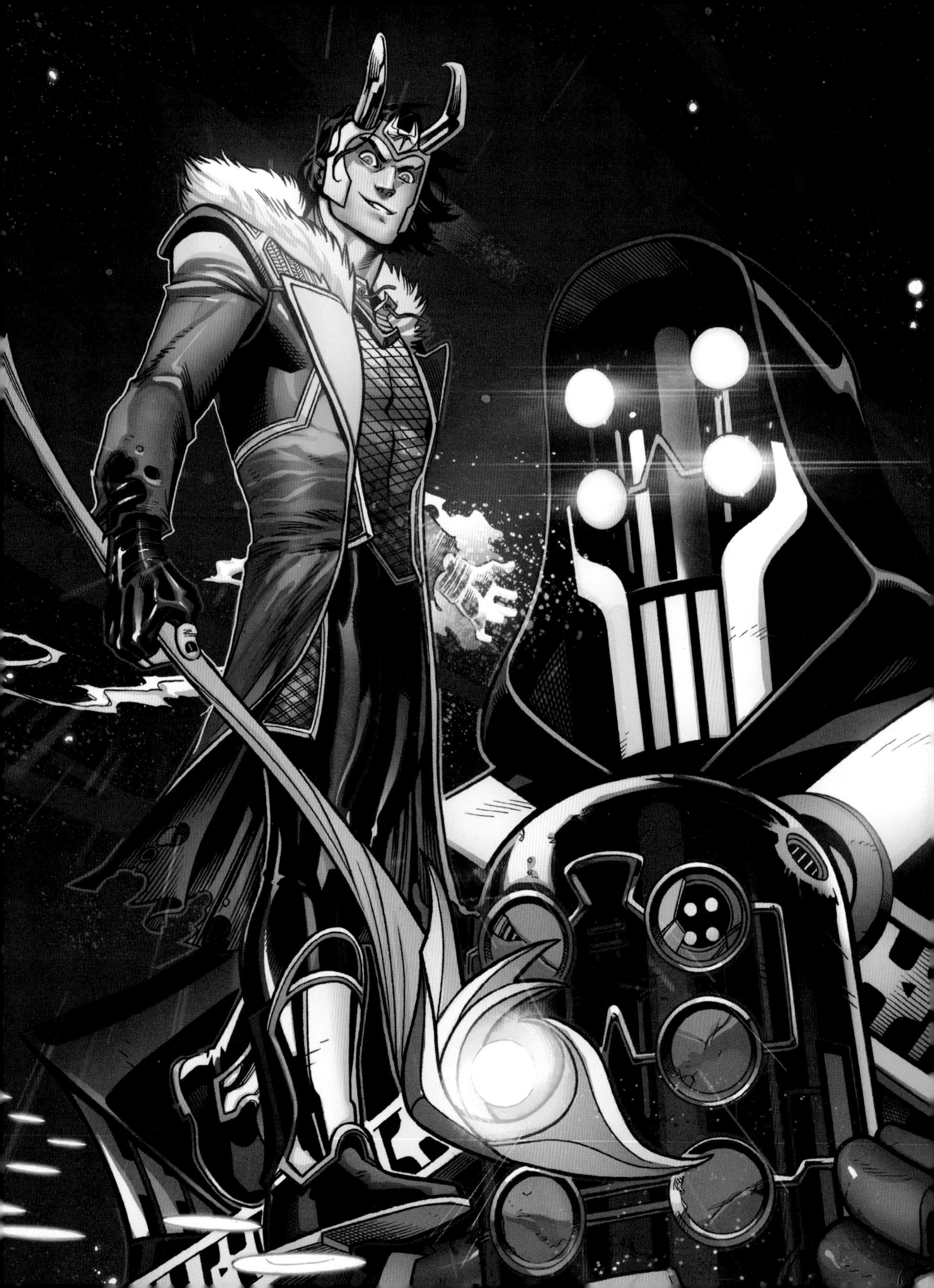

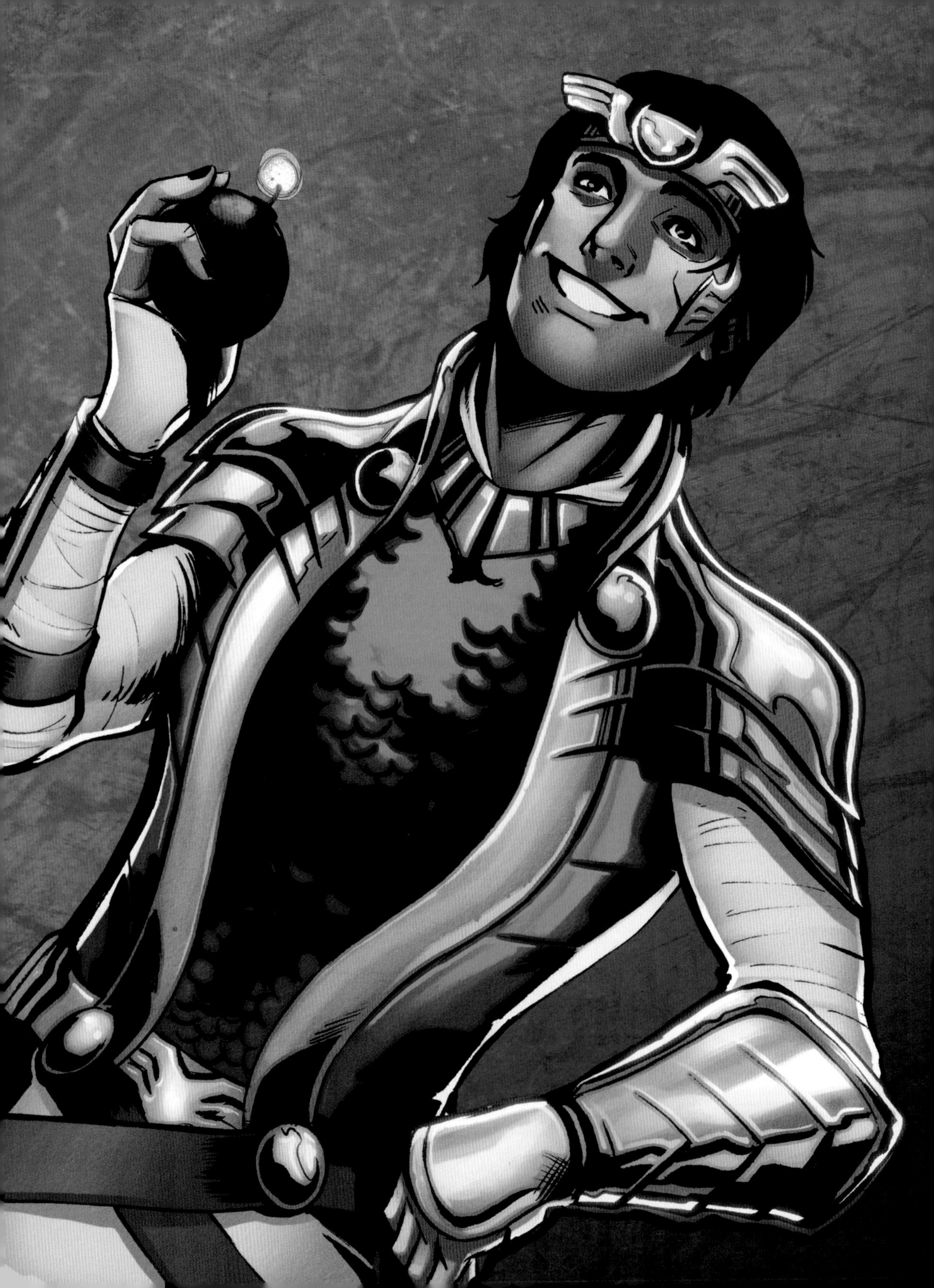

PART 2

The following compilation of tricks seems to target a more experienced version of Loki and build on the basic principles of sorcery. The tricks may need a little more time and practice to master, but they are certainly worth the effort.

—RP

FROM ALL-FATHER TO HALF-FATHER

Your relationship with Odin is . . . complicated. Just when we thought we were done with him, he seems to find a way back. This trick serves as an illustration of our ongoing frustration with the inability of Odin to stay in Hel!

MATERIALS NEEDED

deck of playing cards

scissors

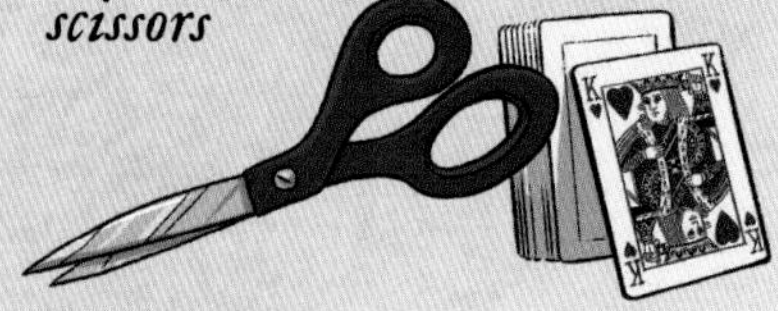

PREPARATION

Use the tip of one of the blades of the scissors to score a horizontal line across the front of the King of Hearts card, about halfway down the card. Be sure not to cut all the way through; the cut should go through just the top layer of the card.

Bend the card a few times to loosen the cut so the card swings back as if on a hinge.

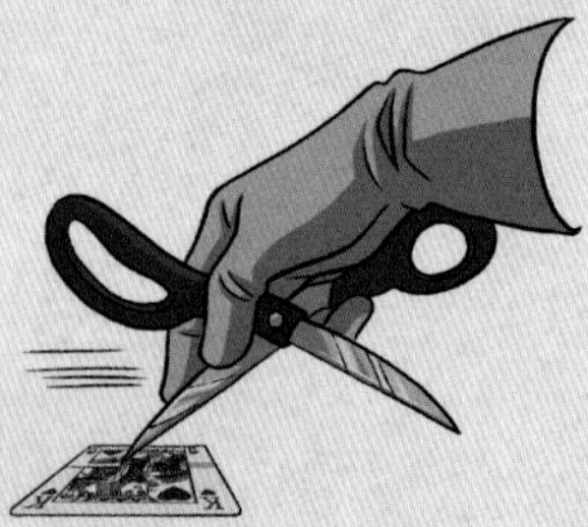

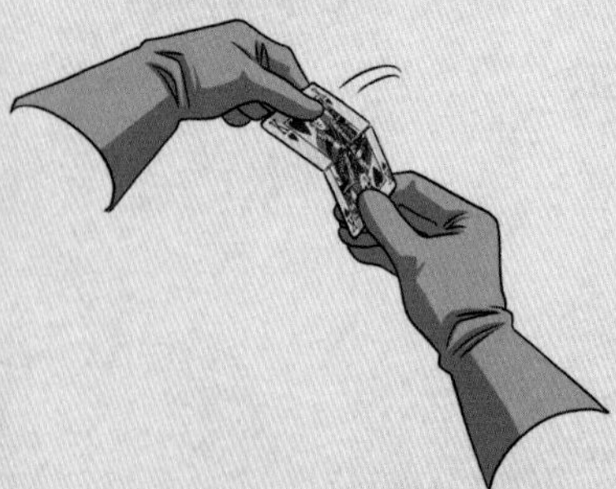

PERFORMANCE

1 Hold your playing card in your right hand (if you have come back from Hel as a leftie, hold it in that hand) with the king side facing the audience. Make sure to prop up the back of the card with your thumb so it does not fall backward along the hinge you have created.

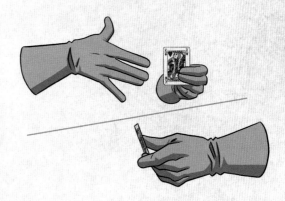

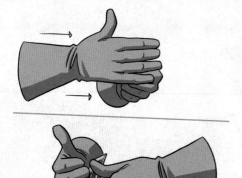

2 Quickly wave your hands up and down as you tell the audience about the great battle of Odin and Surtur during Ragnarok. As you speak of the final blow that felled Odin—with one hand conveniently shielding the card at the most opportune moment—release your thumb and let the top half of the card fall back, so the audience sees that you are now holding only half a king.

3 With another quick flourish of your hands, explain how the All-Father was unexplainably resurrected. As you tell of Odin's return to Asgard, prop up the top half of the card with your thumb again, so the audience now sees the whole of the king.

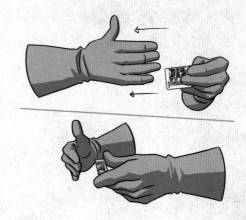

The audience will surely be enchanted by the magic, so feel free to repeat the trick several times while telling tales of the demise and return of Odin. Be sure to end on a half-king as portent to your eventual victory over the All-Father!

VANISHING INFINITY GEMS

Few things in the universe, or the Multiverse, have been as vexing to so many as the Infinity Gems. Created at the beginning of time and coveted by everyone from Thanos to, well, *you*, the Gems seem to be the hardest to find—and keep—of the ancient artifacts. This trick will prove that though the Gems may slip through your fingers, you will always be able to retrieve them.

MATERIALS NEEDED

1 *new box of crayons (preferably six, one for each Infinity Gem)*

scissors

clear tape

1 *large cloth napkin, handkerchief, or bandana*

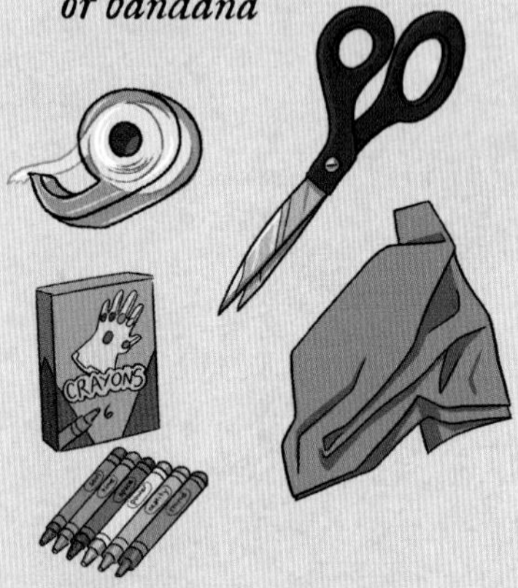
CRAYONS

PREPARATION

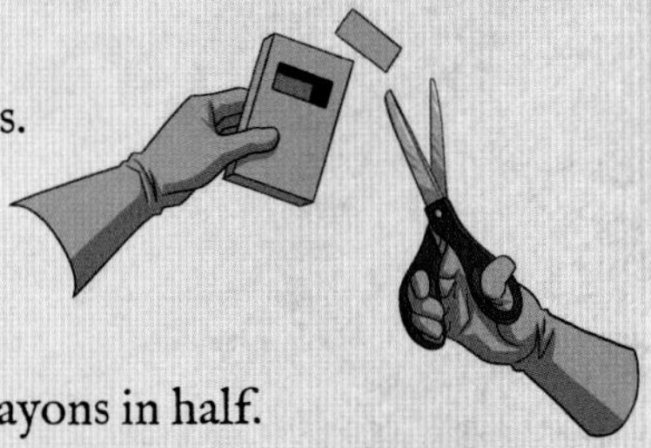

Gently open and empty the box of crayons.

Cut a narrow window at the top of the front of the box to showcase the top half of the crayons.

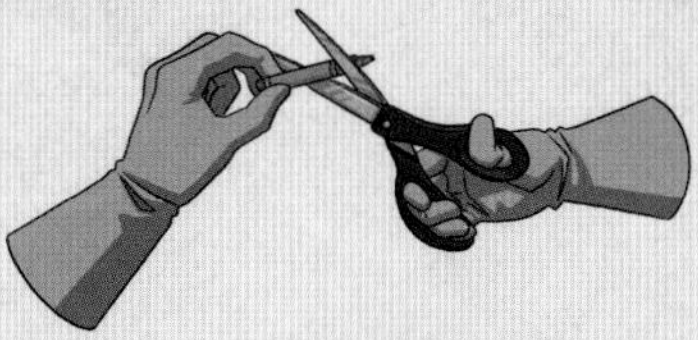

Cut the crayons in half. Place the bottom halves to the side to be used in other mischievous projects, such as creating signs for your magic act or writing up programs.

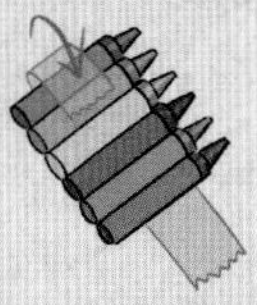

Line up the top halves of the crayons to look as if they are still packaged in the box. Tape the crayons together along their cut edges. Use enough tape to keep the crayons secure, but not too much (or they will not fit back in the box).

Place the taped crayons back into the box. Line up the sharpened points so they can be seen through the window.

Close up the box and tilt it so the crayons slide to the top.

PERFORMANCE

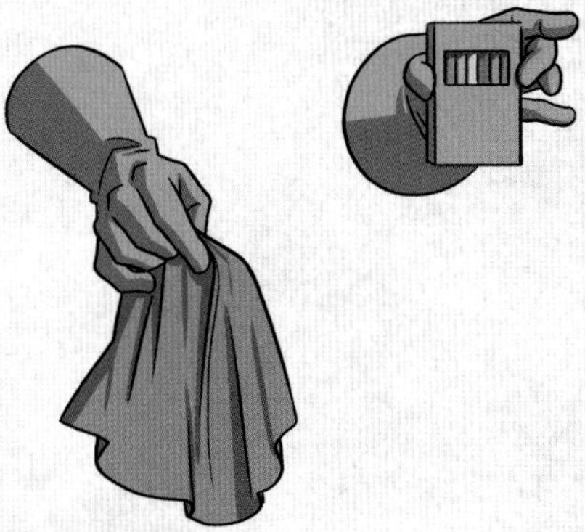

1 Hold up the box of crayons with one hand, pinching the sides with thumb and fingers to hold the crayons in place at the top of the box. Explain to the audience that in all your years, few things in the Multiverse have been as sought after as the fabled Infinity Gems.

CONTINUED . . .

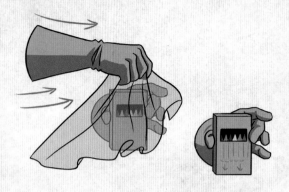

2 Cover the box with the cloth napkin, handkerchief, or bandana with your other hand. As you do so, gently release the pressure of your fingers holding the crayons in place—just enough for the crayons to slip to the bottom of the box (and seem to disappear).

3 Remove the cloth and show the audience the "empty" box. Tell them that the Gems are likely to disappear when least expected.

4 Suggest that you alone have the power to conjure them into and out of your possession. While still holding the sides of the box in your hand, turn the box over by flipping it so the back of the box faces the audience. Rub the back of the box with your other hand theatrically. Meanwhile, when you feel the crayons slip back to the top of the box, tighten the fingers of your hand slightly to hold the crayons in place.

5 Still holding the sides of the box firmly, turn the front of the box toward the audience once more. The crayons will seem to have reappeared.

PENETRATING A SPELL OF PROTECTION

Every member of the Avengers brings their own special set of skills to a fight. But some, like Doctor Strange, bring a little something . . . extra. In fact, the amount of magical energy he imbues into one of his spells of protection pales in comparison to his outsized hubris. This trick will remind any super hero that they can never defeat you.

MATERIALS NEEDED

2 Midgardian coins
1 clear drinking vessel

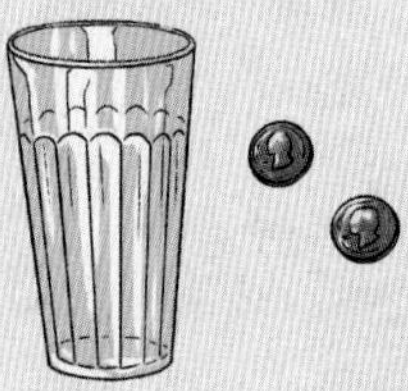

PREPARATION

Pinch one of the coins between where your index and middle fingers meet on your right hand. If you are in alligator form, then tuck it into the scales between two of your digits.

Place the other coin and the drinking vessel on the table in front of you.

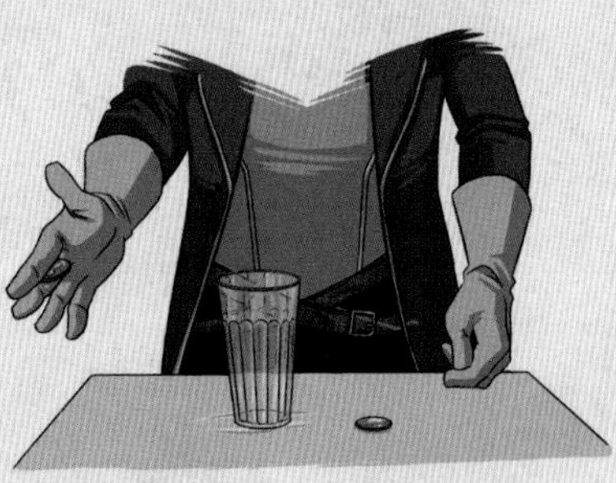

CONTINUED . . .

PERFORMANCE

1 With the coin firmly held between the index and middle fingers of your right hand, hold and pick up the drinking vessel at its opening with your index finger and thumb. Hold it upright so you can easily show the audience its bottom. Describe the vessel as having the same characteristics as one of the protective spells of Doctor Strange.

Use your left index finger and thumb to pick up the other coin.

2 Tap the bottom of the drinking vessel with it, hard and loud enough so the audience can see and hear that the vessel is as solid and clear as any spell formed by the so-called Sorcerer Supreme—and that the coin is as substantial as your far-superior magical skills.

Place the coin back on the table.

3 As you distract the audience by reminding them that you, a Prince of Asgard, cannot be thwarted by any force field, spell, or hex, pretend to pick the coin back up by placing your left index finger on the coin, drag it toward you across the table, and, in as fluid a motion as possible, let it slip off the table onto the floor.

Pinch your left index finger and thumb together to make it look like you are holding the coin again.

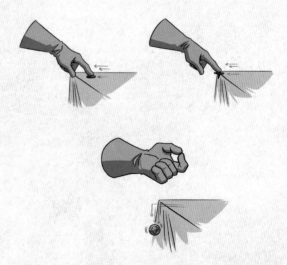

4 Quickly bring those fingers, as if you are still holding the coin, back to the bottom of the drinking vessel and tap its bottom while, at the same time, you release the coin from between your right index and middle fingers, dropping the coin into the drinking vessel. It will seem as though the coin passed through the solid bottom and into the vessel.

5 Rattle the coin theatrically in the drinking vessel, proving to the audience that your cunning, guile, and ability to find the cracks in any spell—or all-too-human Sorcerer Supreme—make you more than capable of defeating any so-called Master of the Mystic Arts.

STIRRING UP CHAOS

Boring can be so . . . boring. Everyone needs a little variety—a little bit of chaos—to make their life worth living. Luckily, you, the God of Mischief, have the ability to stir up just enough confusion and mayhem to keep every realm wondering what is going to happen next.

MATERIALS NEEDED

1 paper, plastic, or lightweight straw

clear double-sided tape

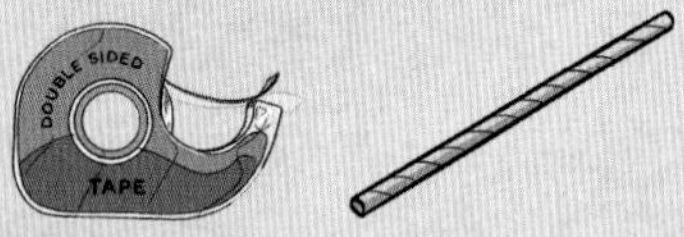
DOUBLE SIDED
TAPE

PREPARATION

Stick a piece of clear double-sided tape to the tip of your left ring finger.

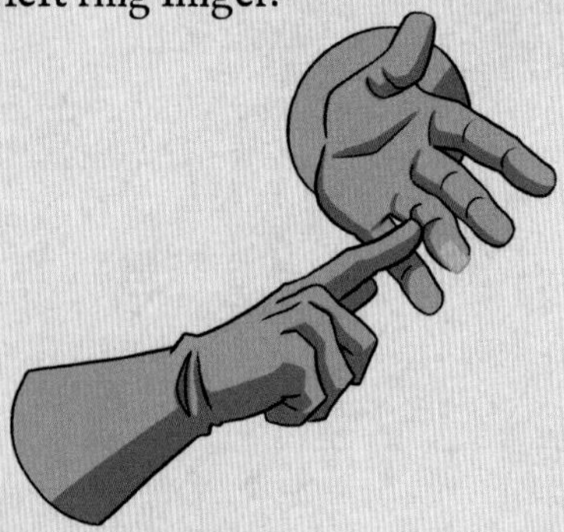

PERFORMANCE

1 Pick up the straw between your right index finger and thumb to show the audience that it is not just an ordinary straw: it is the scepter you wield when you want to make things . . . interesting.

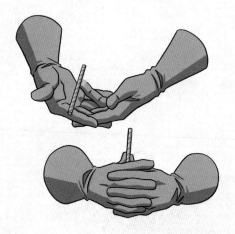

2 Place the straw back on the table and—in one fluid motion—drag it toward you, stick it to the double-sided tape on your left ring finger, and clasp your hands together.

Gently press your thumbs onto the straw so it looks like they are holding it up. Your fingers will look interwoven to the audience, but your left ring finger should be kept free behind the other fingers. Explain that, like your fingers, heroes often come together to foil your plans.

3 Lift your thumbs off the straw. Because the straw is stuck to the tape on your finger, it will appear to be standing on its own. Remind the audience that you do not need a team behind you.

4 Wiggle your ring finger behind your hands—and the straw will appear to move of its own volition. Explain to the audience that this shows how your power will keep stirring up chaos and sowing disbelief, in this or any realm, for all eternity.

THE HEX OF THE SCARLET WITCH

The universe is filled with sorcerers, magicians, and witches. Far too many, really. One of the most famous magic wielders, the Scarlet Witch, has the ability to affect probability. She may be well known, but everyone should also know that anything she can do, you can do better!

MATERIALS NEEDED

1 white die with black dots

1 black marker

6 4 x 5 inch index cards (thick enough for a marker not to bleed through)

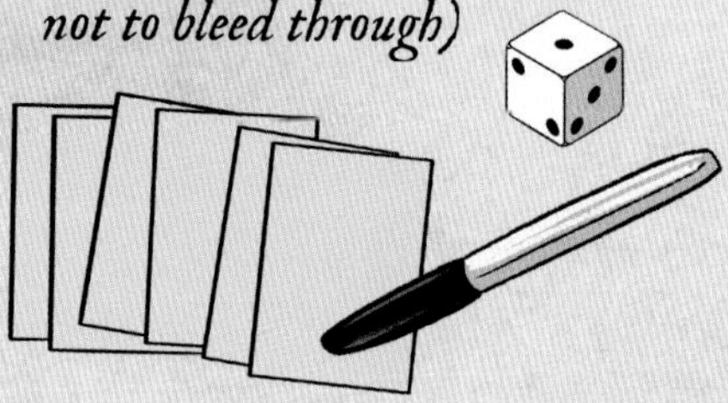

PREPARATION

Use the black marker to color a third dot onto the 2-side of the die, so the die has two 3-sides.

Write numbers 1 through 6 on the front of the index cards.

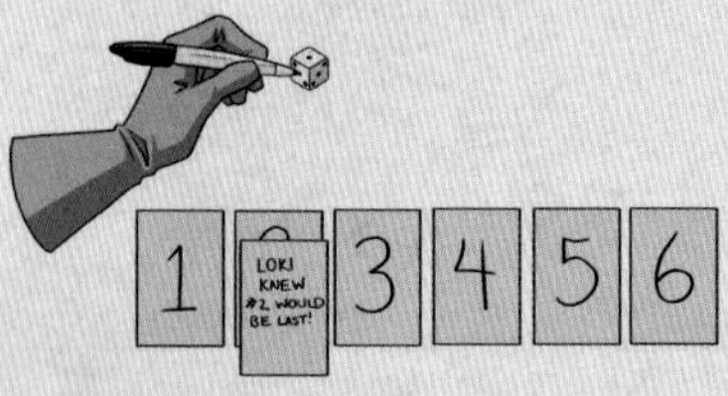
1
LOKI KNEW #2 WOULD BE LAST!
3
4
5
6

Write "Loki knew #2 would be last!" on the back of the number 2 card.

PERFORMANCE

1 Lay the cards out on the table so the audience can clearly see the numbers. Describe how the Scarlet Witch uses her powers to try to get her way—and how you use your far-superior skills to get *your* way.

2 Invite a member of the audience to roll the die. Tell them that—as a mere mortal—they (like Wanda Maximoff) have no true say in what happens.

3 Remove the card corresponding to whichever number comes up. For example, if someone rolls a 5 on the die, take away the index card labeled with the number 5.

4 Continue to let them roll, taking away the cards until only one is left: the index card that is number 2.

Turn the number 2 card over, showing them that your spells can match—and defeat—any hex of the Scarlet Witch.

HIDE-AND-SEEK

One of the best parts of doing something bad is not getting caught! This trick reminds the audience, your brother, his friends, and anyone within any of the Ten Realms that you, your magic, and your mischief are uncontainable!

MATERIALS NEEDED

4 playing cards including the Jack of Diamonds and the Ten of Clubs

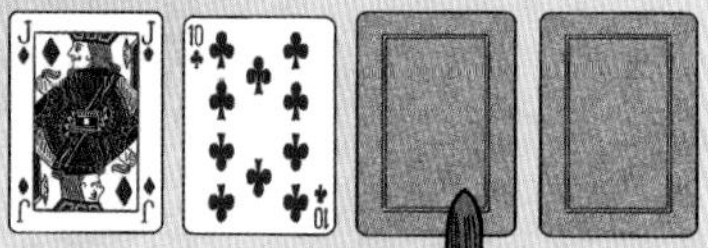

clear double-sided tape or glue

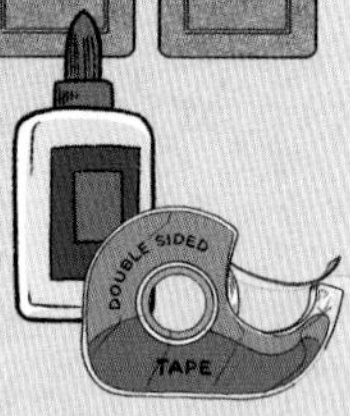
DOUBLE SIDED
TAPE

PREPARATION

Tape or glue the backs of the Jack of Diamonds and the Ten of Clubs together. This creates one "double-faced" card.

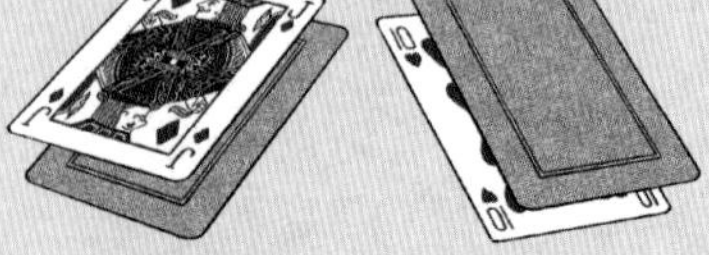

Tape or glue the faces of the other two cards together. This creates one "double-backed" card.

PERFORMANCE

1 Explain that the so-called forces of good have been trying—in vain—for centuries to rein in your mischief. And though some may get tired of this sort of endless game of hide-and-seek, you are just getting started. Pick up both cards between the thumb and index finger of your right hand.

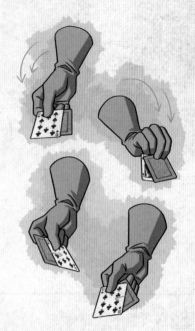

Gently slide the cards from left to right as you turn your hand front to back. The audience will think that they are seeing two regular cards, each with a front and back. Explain that you are represented by the Jack of Diamonds, and the Ten of Clubs represents the number of realms trying to confine your chaos—and continue to turn your hand around and move your fingers back and forth to create extra movement and delightful confusion!

2 Bring your hands together in front of you. Open the fingers of your right hand and show, as if by accident, the Ten of Clubs side of the double-faced card. Use your right hand to bring that card behind your back, still holding the double-backed card in your left hand.

Ask the audience where your card is, the Jack of Diamonds. Since the audience watched you place the Ten of Clubs behind your back, they will naturally think that the card in front of you in your left hand is the Loki card.

Laugh at them when they point to the card in front of you.

3 Bring your right hand from behind your back, making sure that the Jack of Diamonds side faces the now-stunned audience.

Remind them that though you may be sought, you can never be found.

POWER OVER THE ELEMENTS

One does not need to be an Atlantean, a mutant, or even an Odinson to wield the power of hydrokinesis. Water will bend to your will as effortlessly as any other natural (or unnatural) element will. But since throwing rocks at your audience can be frowned upon as much as depriving them of air or setting your stage on fire, it is best to give them just a taste of what you can do.

MATERIALS NEEDED

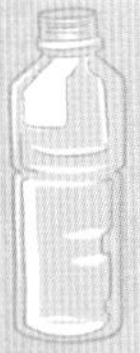

1 clear plastic bottle

1 black marker

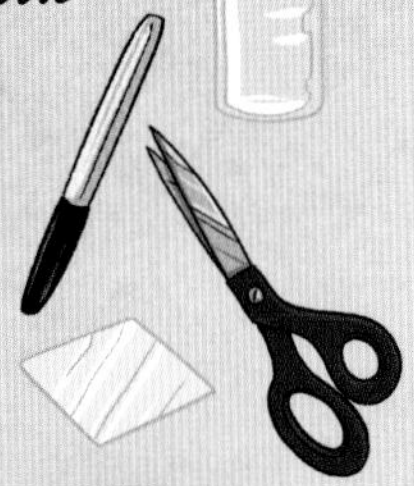

water (enough to fill the bottle)

1 piece of thin clear plastic

scissors

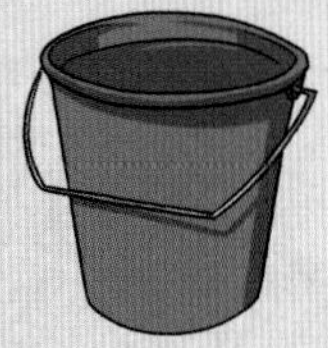

large bucket or bowl

PREPARATION

Place the mouth of the empty bottle on top of the plastic. Use the marker to trace around the opening. Use the scissors to cut the circle you created out of the plastic. The circular disc of plastic should completely cover the mouth of the bottle.

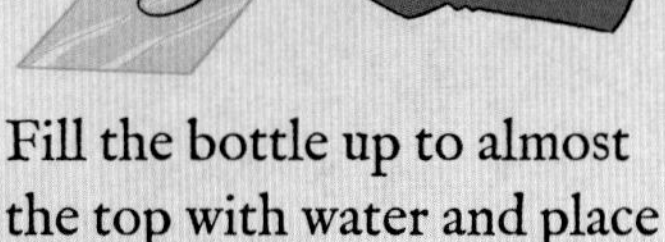

Fill the bottle up to almost the top with water and place the plastic disc on top.

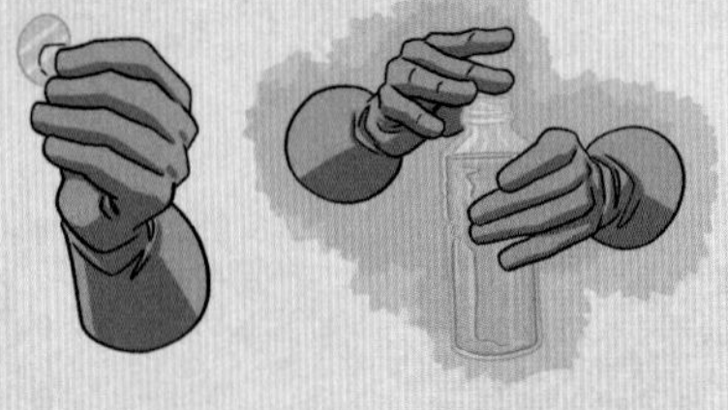

PERFORMANCE

1 Pick up the bottle—without squeezing it—in your left hand and hold it over the bucket or bowl.

In one fluid motion, place your right index finger firmly on top of the disc and turn the bottle upside down.

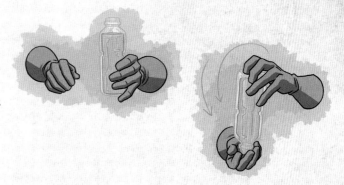

2 Continue to hold the bottle upside down, and remove your finger by lifting it straight down and away from the disk—do not slide your finger off it. The hydrostatic pressure will hold the plastic disc on the mouth of the bottle. Explain to your audience how you have the power to control the forces of gravity and hold back the tides.

3 But you can also, if you so choose, release those forces to wreak havoc. To demonstrate, snap the fingers of one hand and slightly squeeze the bottle with your other hand. The pressure will release the fluid down into the bucket.

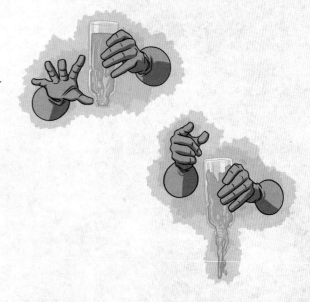

VANISHING DAGGER

Your cunning and guile will get you far, but there is nothing quite like adding an element of surprise. Especially when the surprise is weaponry.

MATERIALS NEEDED

1 *toothpick or coffee stirrer*

scissors

clear double-sided tape

DOUBLE SIDED
TAPE

PREPARATION

Use the scissors to trim the toothpick or stirrer to about 1½ inches long.

Attach the toothpick or stirrer to the back of your right thumb with a piece of double-sided tape. The toothpick or stirrer should extend past your thumb a little more than an inch.

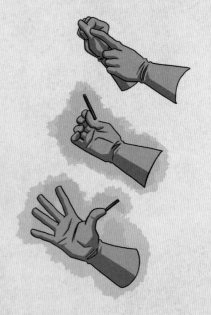

PERFORMANCE

1 Pinch the thumb and index finger of your right hand together and extend the hand to the audience. It will look, from their perspective, as if you are holding the toothpick or stirrer up between your thumb and index finger. Tell the audience that though you are currently without a dagger, what you hold before them can be as deadly a weapon when put into the right hands. *Your* hands.

2 But weapons can sometimes be detected by Midgardian technology, so you have found that secreting them away can be to your advantage. On the count of three, open your hand and raise it up, stretching and extending your thumb away from the audience and toward you. The toothpick or stirrer will seem to have disappeared.

3 Identify a possible threat in the audience, and, on the count of three, summon your dagger by bringing your hand back to the original position. The toothpick or stirrer will reappear.

YGGDRASIL: THE WORLD TREE

As a child, you learned that your home of Asgard was cosmically and eternally connected to the nine other realms: Midgard, Jotunheim, Svartalfheim, Vanaheim, Nidavellir, Niflheim, Muspelheim, Alfheim, and Heven via the complex tapestry of universe-spanning branches of Yggdrasil, the World Tree. And as you grew, you grew to understand that you, as son of Jotenheim, a prince of Asgard, and conqueror of Midgard, could—and should—be the one to rule over them all.

MATERIALS NEEDED

10 11 x 17 *inch pages of newspaper or other thin paper*

1 *rubber band*

scissors

PREPARATION

Set one sheet of newspaper aside.

Loosely roll another sheet of paper, starting at the shorter (11 inch) side until 5 or 6 inches remain at the end.

Insert another sheet of newspaper into the roll, overlapping with the last piece of paper, and loosely roll that one until you have 5 or 6 inches at the end.

Keep inserting more sheets of newspaper and loosely rolling, one by one.

Place a rubber band around the middle of the rolled-up tube of nine pieces of newspaper to keep it from unrolling.

Use the scissors to cut four slits from one end of the tube to almost its middle, about ⅓ of the way down. The tube should have four branches above the rubber band and remain intact below it.

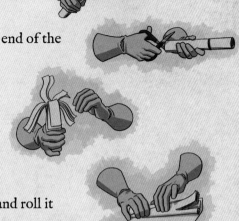

Remove the rubber band and unroll the tube only until about 3 or 4 inches of the last sheet is exposed.

Insert the remaining sheet of newspaper and roll it around the tube to hide the four slits.

Replace the rubber band around the tube to hold all the sheets in place. It should look as if the tube is totally intact.

PERFORMANCE

1 Hold the rolled-up paper tube, representing Yggdrasil, vertically in your left hand. With your right hand, reach into the tube, pinch one of the pre-cut four branches between your thumb and forefinger, and pull down, tearing the outside sheet along the pre-cut edges. Assign the realms of Midgard (as a courtesy to your current situation), Jotunheim, the place of your birth, and Heven, the newly discovered realm, to this branch.

Repeat three more times, assigning a branch to Svartalfheim and Vanaheim, then Nidavellir and Niflheim, and lastly Muspelheim and Alfheim.

CONTINUED . . .

2 Reach again into the tube and pinch the corner of the innermost piece of paper between your thumb and forefinger. Remind the audience that you are an Asgardian.

Gripping the tube firmly with your other hand, gently tug on the corner and pull it out of the tube. And say you should be the rightful ruler of all ten realms.

3 Continue to pull, and Yggdrasil will continue to grow and flourish. When you get to the full height of the tree, point it toward the audience. Describe how you will rule with wisdom and kindness—as long as you are obeyed.

Crush the paper between your hands to demonstrate the consequences if you are opposed.

MATERIALS NEEDED

Midgardian paper currency (dollar bill)

2 identical decks of playing cards

scissors

glue or clear double-sided tape

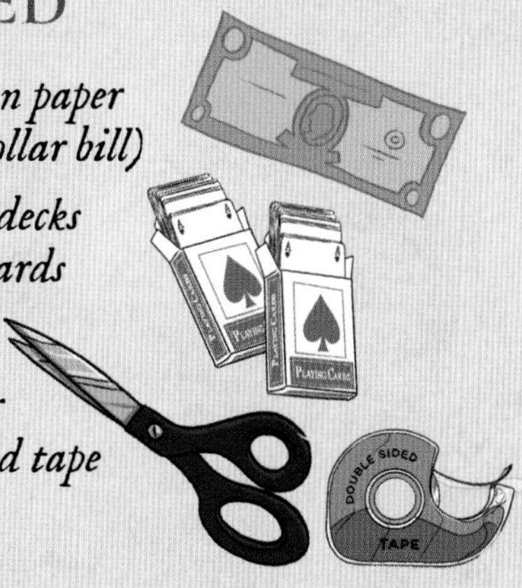
DOUBLE SIDED
TAPE

PREPARATION

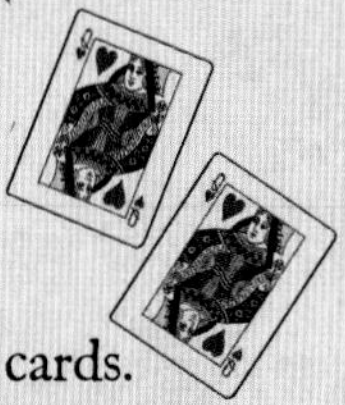

Remove the two Queens of Hearts from the decks.

Use the scissors to cut the bottom third off one of the cards.

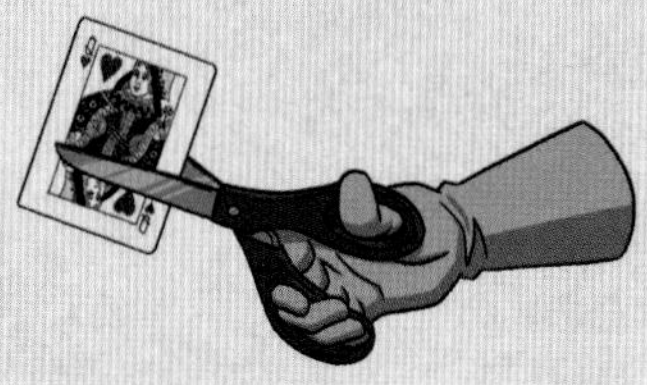

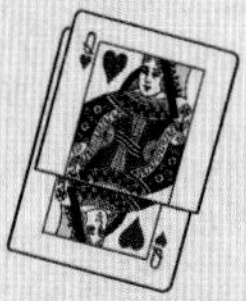

Lay the two Queens faceup. And then place the shorter Queen of Hearts directly on top of the complete Queen of Hearts. Line them up so their top and side edges match.

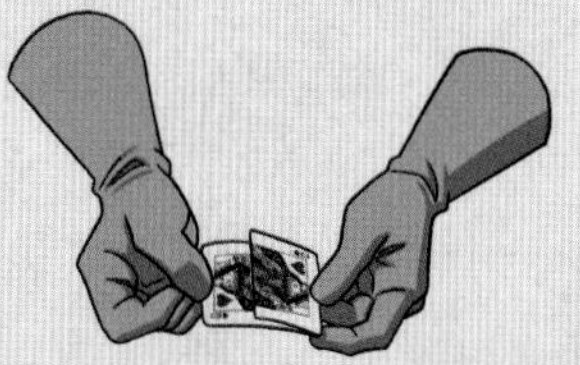

Glue or tape just a bit of the top of the face of the shorter card onto the top of the face of the complete card. This will connect the tops of both cards and create a hinge, with the short card acting as a flap.

ODIN AND FRIGGA

Every family is complicated. And yours is no exception. When you were not in conflict with your parents, Odin and Frigga, they often were in conflict with each other. This trick demonstrates that your parents have, for millennia, orbited around each other, as connected on ideological issues as they were divided on strategic courses of action, and always—*always*—incapable of understanding or appreciating you.

CONTINUED . . .

PERFORMANCE

1 Hold the dollar bill for the audience to see. Point out to them the physical resemblance between George Washington and the All-Father. Fold the dollar bill lengthwise in half. The crease should be at the bottom with the two open edges at the top, like a "V."

2 Hold its left edge between the thumb and middle finger of your left hand.

Hold the face of the prepared card up to the audience with your right hand. Point out the resemblance between the Queen and the All-Mother. Pretend to slip the prepared card into the folded dollar bill. Make sure that only the front flap, the shorter top card, will slip into the "V." The complete card should slip behind the bill, but its bottom edge should not yet be seen by the audience.

3 Grip the right side of the folded bill between your right thumb and middle finger. Rest each of your index fingers on the top edge of the card, just as your parents have tried to manipulate you.

4 Tap the card down gently down, so the audience begins to see the bottom of the complete card slide beneath the bill. The back half of the bill should slip under the flap of the prepared card, keeping the card in place. Keep tapping until the bottom edge of the short top card meets the fold of the bill. While the audience sees what appears to be the card going through the bill, point out this representation of the tumultuous union of Odin and Frigga.

Use your index fingers to slide the card back and forth along the length of the bill—just as your parents often pushed you around—demonstrating how the card seems to be floating freely.

5 But, as any child will, you have grown tired of their tricks, so end this one. Push a finger between the halves of the bill and place your finger over the bottom edge of the cut card (so the audience does not see the edge). and slide the card off the bill. The card and bill are—like your parents—now fully separate.

Place the card facedown on the table to hide the cut edge—and unfold the bill to show that it is whole, as you will be . . . once you regain your magic, and reclaim your place in the universe.

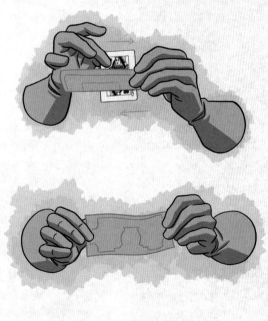

THE FROZEN PLAINS OF JOTUNHEIM

No matter how comfortable you may feel in the warm verdant meadows of Asgard, someone will always want to remind you that you were adopted (stolen?) from the icy vasts of Jotunheim. This trick reminds the audience that you know exactly where you come from, where you are, and where you want to be.

MATERIALS NEEDED

opaque drinking vessel
clear drinking vessel
small sponge
ice cubes
water

PREPARATION

Push the sponge into the opaque drinking vessel. Place ice cubes on top of the sponge.

Pour about 1 inch of water into the clear drinking vessel.

PERFORMANCE

1 Hold the opaque drinking vessel in one hand and the clear one in the other.

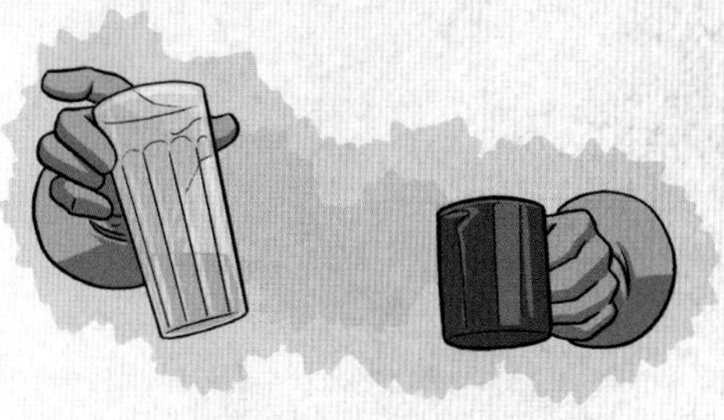

Gently swish the water in the clear vessel around, suggesting it flows like those in the rivers and streams of Asgard.

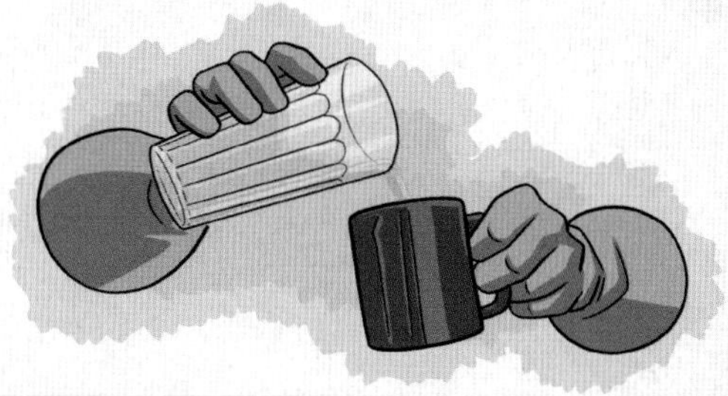

2 As you compare and contrast the climates and terrains of Asgard and Jotunheim, pour the water from the clear vessel into the opaque vessel.

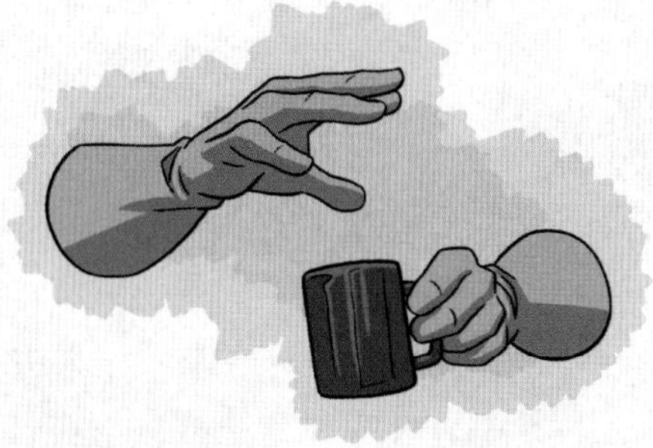

Whisper a few magic words in ancient Jotun into the opaque vessel—slowly enough to give the sponge time to absorb the water.

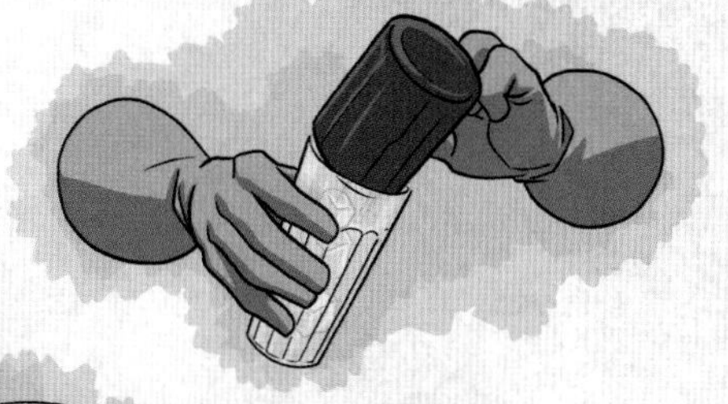

3 As proof that you are still a Frost Giant to be reckoned with, tip the opaque vessel over the clear one, pouring the ice cubes into it.

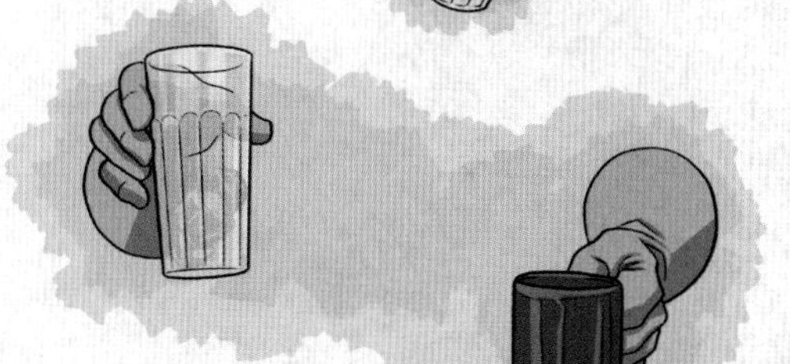

BOTTLING UP THOR

As important as it is for you to regain your full magical abilities, it is also vitally important that you recall the good times—especially the ones that were particularly humiliating for Thor. This trick should bring back happy memories of when you turned your brother into a frog.

MATERIALS NEEDED

2-liter plastic bottle
scissors
fork
lime

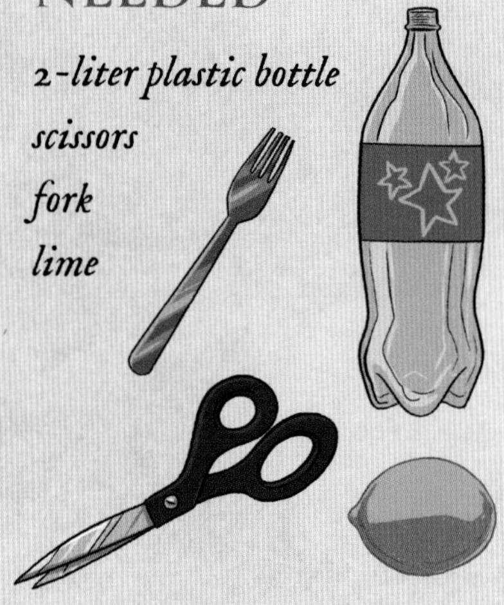

PREPARATION

Use the scissors to cut a piece out of the top part of the bottle, from just below the neck of the bottle to about one-third down its side. It should be large enough to fit the lime, but small enough not to be seen from the sides by the audience.

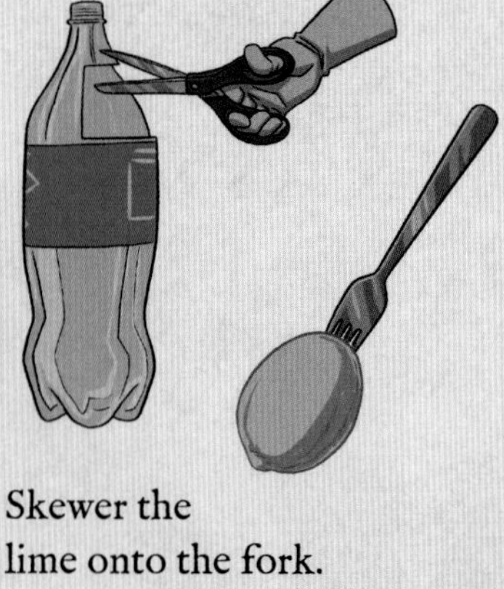

Skewer the lime onto the fork.

PERFORMANCE

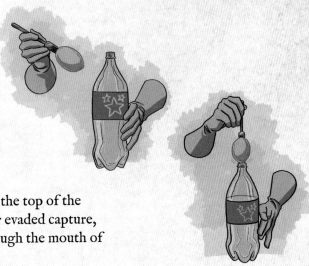

1 Tell the audience to prepare to hear about the time you magically transformed Thor into a frog as green as the lime you have stuck on the end of the fork.

Once you stop laughing, unscrew the top of the bottle. Show how, much like Thor evaded capture, the skewered lime will not fit through the mouth of the bottle.

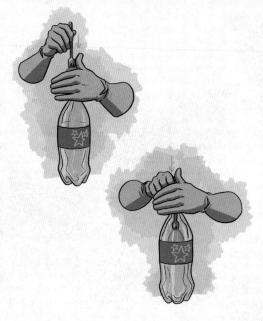

2 Hold your hand in front of the mouth of the bottle, shielding the lime as well. As you whisper a few magical words, remind the audience that there was once another powerful frog in the Multiverse: Throg, also known as Simon Walterson or Puddlegulp. Move the lime back toward you slightly so it is now above the hole in the back of the bottle.

Lower the skewered lime into the hole. The audience will see the lime enter the bottle, proving that the might—and size— of Thor is no match for your magic.

Move the skewered lime up and down to show that it is in the bottle.

3 Return your hand to the mouth of the bottle to shield that you are pulling the lime out of the back opening. Announce that this proves that you are willing to show mercy to your brother, whatever form he may take.

DIVIDED THEY FALL

The Avengers present themselves as a solid and unified group. But you know better, do you not? For behind their carefully crafted public image, you know that they are in fact composed of individuals who fight amongst themselves as often as they fight you. This trick shows the world who they *really* are.

MATERIALS NEEDED

banana
toothpick

PREPARATION

Poke the toothpick through the skin of the banana, about 2 inches from the top.

Slowly and gently push the toothpick until you can feel the point just starting to poke through the opposite side of the banana. Do not let it come through.

Without removing it from the hole, wiggle the toothpick inside the banana, back and forth, right to left, a couple of times.

Repeat about an inch lower on the banana and repeat again until you have stuck the toothpick into the banana a total of five times.

PERFORMANCE

1 While holding it for the audience to see, suggest that the Avengers appear to be as natural, full of energy, and, especially, whole as the banana.

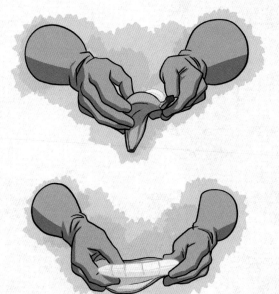

2 Unpeel the banana to show not only that each of the original Avengers is represented—Iron Man, Thor, Wasp, Ant-Man, and the Hulk—but also that they are a team as naturally divided as they are false.

3 Take a bite out of one of the pieces and savor your victory.

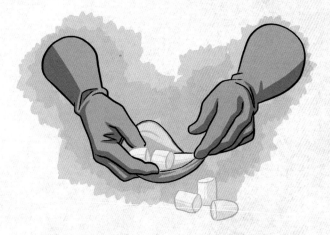

YOU ARE LOKI

You are a Prince of Asgard, the rightful heir to Jotunheim. You have been, at one time or another, and at the same time, old, young, male, female, a myth, a legend, a friend, an enemy, and a brother. Living through multiple timelines can get . . . confusing. But who are you?

MATERIALS NEEDED

1 *piece of string, about 60 inches long*

1 *plastic straw*

scissors

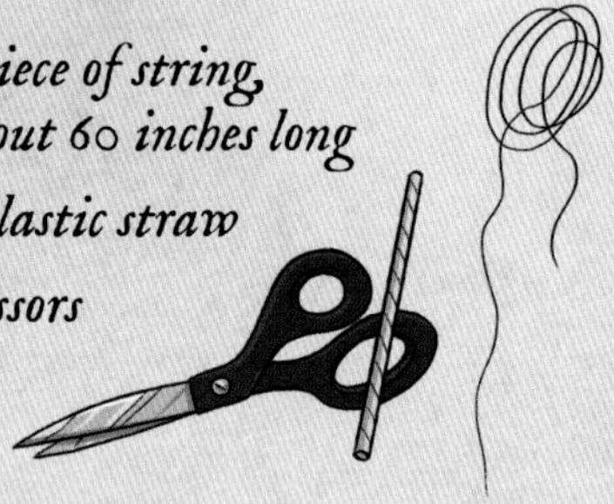

PREPARATION

Lay the straw on the table.

Use the tip of the scissors to carefully cut a 3-inch long slit at the center of the straw.

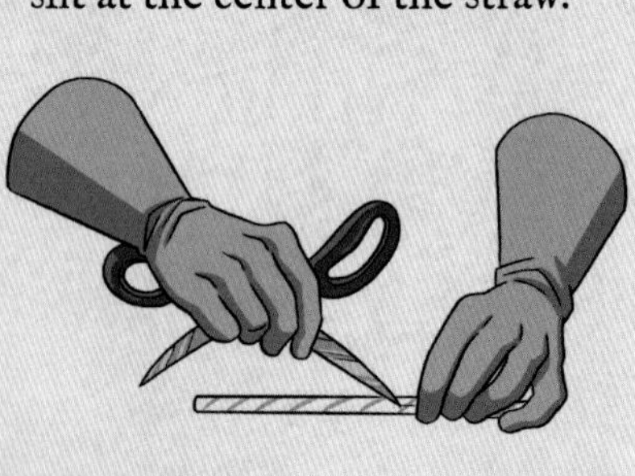

PERFORMANCE

1 Show the audience the string, symbolizing the entirety of your own (finite) life's experiences. Use the scissors to cut it in half.

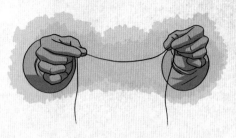

Place one half of the string, which symbolizes all of the things you would rather forget (or not want anyone to know), to the side.

Lift the other string, which symbolizes the triumphs and tricks you want to remember (and which you want everyone to know).

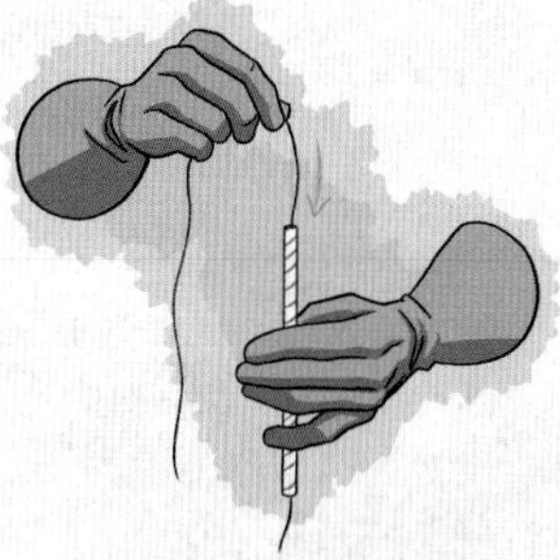

2 Thread the string through the straw—reminiscent of how your life is threaded through multiple realities and timelines—until you see both ends of the string coming out of the straw at about the same length.

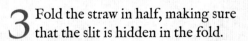

Pull on the dangling ends of the string, one and then the other, to prove to the audience that the string is whole.

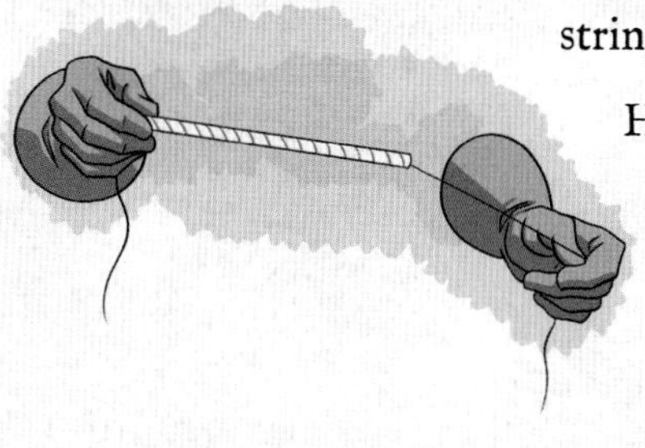

Hold the straw with two hands, one hand on each half of the straw. The slit should face downward.

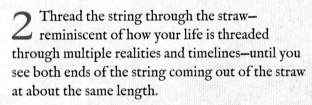

3 Fold the straw in half, making sure that the slit is hidden in the fold.

Hold the folded straw with your left fist, with its bent top clearly visible to the audience. Your fingers should cover the two halves of the straw below the fold.

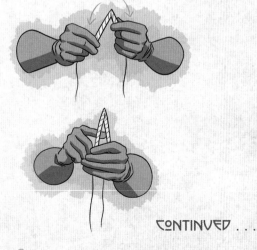

CONTINUED . . .

With your right hand, pull on one and then the other of the dangling strings to show the audience that the string is still whole.

Then tug on both ends of the string at once. This will pull the center section of the string through the slit and away from the folded part of the straw—still hidden in your left fist.

4 Use your right hand to pick up the scissors and cut through the top of the straw (as any of your enemies might try to sabotage your journey through time and space). With your right hand, spread apart the tops of the halves of the straw to show the audience that it is indeed cut completely in two.

Use your right hand to pull on one end of the dangling string, and then the other, to show the audience that the string is still connected.

5 Line up the two halves of straw again, holding it loosely in your left hand.

With your right hand, pull the string completely out of the straw. Show the audience that the string, unlike the straw, is still whole, thanks to you.

Set the two pieces of the straw and the whole piece of string on the table. You have proven that not only will you live to fight another day but that of all things you are—of all titles, of all the lives you lived and will live—one thing is forever constant: You. Are. Loki.

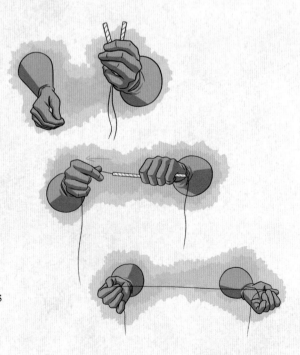

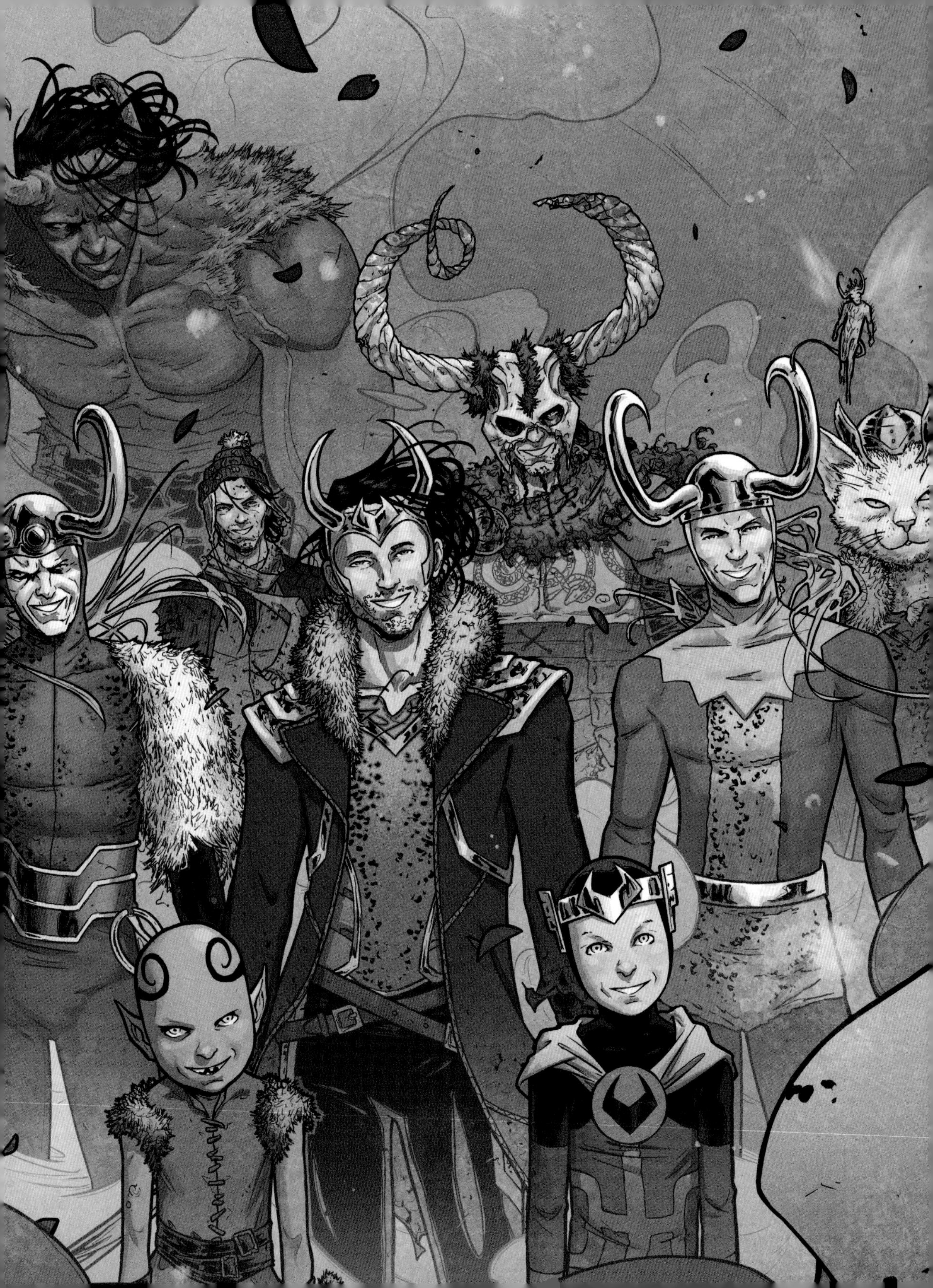

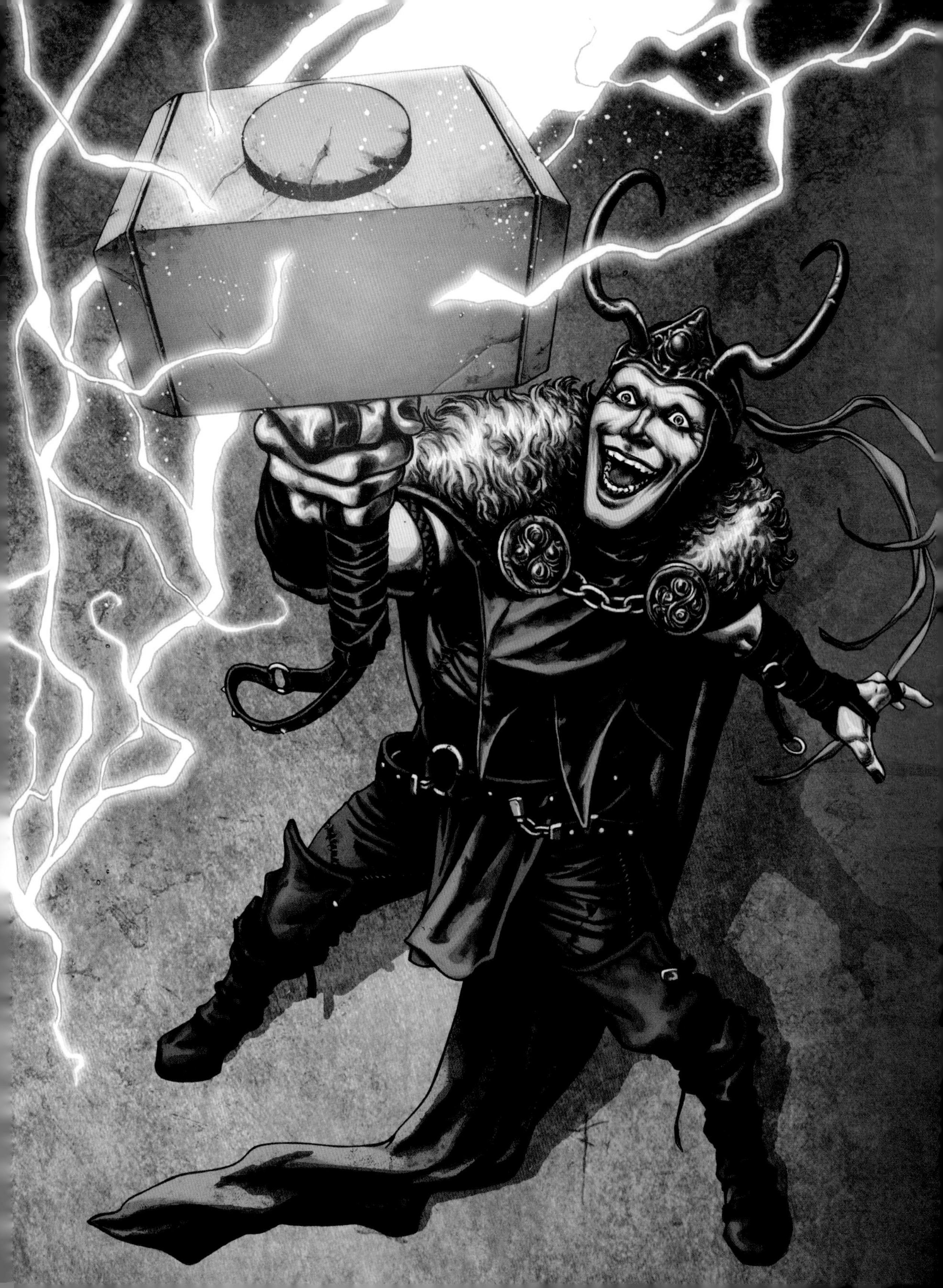

PART 3

These tricks appear to target
the most seasoned, diabolical, and
mischievous version of Loki.

—RP

YOUR MIGHTY SCEPTER

Some humans need an iron suit or a shield to be a hero. Some villains need a dose of radiation or mechanical tentacles to wreak havoc. But you? You do not really need any accessories to be the best. Though your scepter does add a bit of drama!

MATERIALS NEEDED

Midgardian paper currency (dollar bill)

a small Midgardian coin, like a penny

rubber band

PREPARATION

Pinch the penny or small coin between the thumb and index finger of your left hand.

PERFORMANCE

1 While pinching the coin between the thumb and index finger of your left hand, hold up the dollar bill (lengthwise) to the audience so they can see the bill.

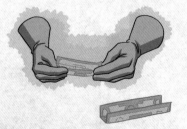

2 Slowly fold the bill in thirds horizontally by folding the top third of the bill down and toward you, and then folding the bottom third up and toward you. Explain to the audience that your skills as a magic wielder are as expansive as all of creation. But sometimes it is nice to have a scepter to help you focus your power.

3 As you fold, secretly slip the penny into the crease created in the dollar bill. The folded bill is now narrow, resembling your mighty scepter.

4 Gently tilt the bill toward your right so the penny is close to the farthest edge in the crease.

Adjust the placement of the bill on your right middle finger until you feel the penny weighing it down (acting as a counterweight).

Once it feels secure, slowly move your left middle finger away from the bill. The bill will appear to be floating on your finger.

5 Pick up the rubber band with your left hand and slip it around the end of the bill, working it all the way past your finger on the right. Explain that this shows how you can use your scepter to channel your enormous power. Place the rubber band back on the table.

6 Tilt the bill so the penny escapes into your right palm and unfold the bill, reminding the audience that your scepter is nothing without you.

7 With the penny hidden in your right palm, hold up the unfolded, ordinary bill. Bow deeply, with the knowledge that true power lies within you.

THE SHIELD

Midgardians believe they live in a world of men, monsters, and gods. But you, Loki, know that the Multiverse contains a multitude of beings and forces that their small minds could never comprehend. Some are beyond even your understanding, like the shield owned by Captain America, which defies natural—and unnatural—laws of physics. So, rather than trying to comprehend how it gets from one place to another and back into Captain America's self-righteous possession, the only thing you can do is to deflect it or try to contain it.

MATERIALS NEEDED

1 *large Midgardian coin*
clear double-sided tape

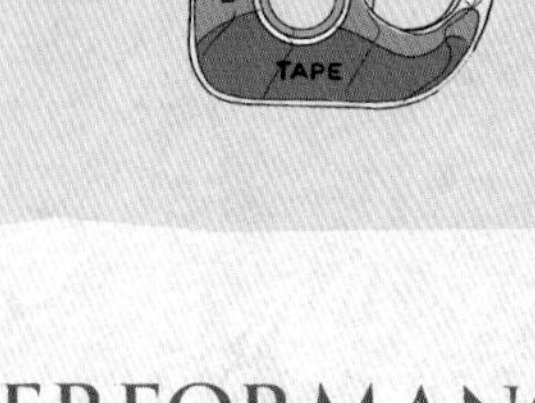

PREPARATION

Place a small piece of double-sided tape on the back of your left hand, between your thumb and forefinger.

PERFORMANCE

1 Show the audience that both of your hands are empty because, unlike the artificially enhanced Star-Spangled Man, you have no need for accessories.

Pinch the coin, representing the prized shield of Captain America, between the thumb and forefinger of your right hand.

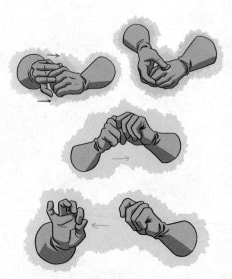

2 Move your hands together so it looks as if you are pushing the coin inside your left hand with your right index finger. You will actually be sliding it onto the back of your left hand and pressing it onto the double-sided tape with your thumb.

Theatrically squeeze both hands together, describing how the shield seems to disregard any of the rules of physics.

With both hands in fists, move your hands apart while explaining that though you may not always be able to deflect the shield with your physical being, you can certainly teleport it away from you.

3 Slowly and dramatically open the fingers in your right hand to show that the coin is not there. No Earthly trinket could ever be a threat to you.

Slowly and dramatically open the fingers in your left hand to show that the coin is not there either. Pause for a moment to laugh at their Midgardian folly.

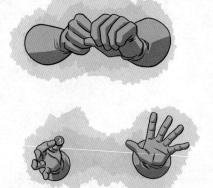

4 But because you are a benevolent god, you are willing to retrieve the toy of the Captain from the abyss. Close your left hand again into a fist.

Reach into your left fist with your right index finger.

With your right thumb, gently pull the coin off the tape and pinch it between your thumb and forefinger again.

Gently pull out the coin and toss it into the crowd, telling them to return the shield to the Captain . . . if he ever again dares to show his masked face in your presence.

RISE ABOVE IT ALL

Many species marvel at those who can break free of gravity and fly through the sky. As if it is hard. This trick demonstrates that your abilities allow you to traverse space, time, and the atmosphere. All without a hammer dragging you along the way.

MATERIALS NEEDED

1 *pair of lightweight slip-on shoes or slippers*

2 *medium binder clips*

1 *blanket or bedsheet long enough to go from your waist to the ground*

PREPARATION

Use the binder clips to fasten the slip-on shoes together near the back.

Slip your right foot fully into one shoe.

Slip your left foot only part of the way into the other shoe.

PERFORMANCE

1 Stand before the audience with your arms outstretched so they can see that you have no special apparatus or shoes. Allow them to bow, genuflect, or otherwise pay tribute to your greatness.

2 In one fluid motion, hold the blanket or sheet at waist height in front of you and bend your knees very slightly—just enough so that to the audience you appear to be the same height (though now you are a little shorter). Make sure the toes of your shoes are still visible from beneath the blanket.

3 As you mock your brother for needing props to hurdle through air and space, gently slip your right foot out of its shoe and place it behind your left foot. Take a moment to position it so you can balance and feel steady and secure.

4 Slowly straighten your right leg as you raise the blanket (and lift your left foot and the shoes at the same speed you are raising the blanket). The clipped-together shoes will look as if they are levitating beneath the blanket. Remind the Midgardians that they should always—always—look up to you.

5 Still balanced on your right foot, tilt your body and your left foot (with the shoes) to show how you can also maneuver in the air.

6 Slowly lower the blanket and your left foot at the same speed. Slip your right foot back into its shoe.

Cast away the blanket to reveal your feet, firmly back on the ground. Demand applause.

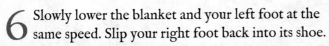

HEIMDALL AND THE BIFROST

For millennia, Heimdall, Guardian of the Bifrost, has protected Asgard from invaders, enemies, and unwanted guests. Heimdall serves as a powerful protector of the realm. No one gets past Heimdall. Well, except for you.

MATERIALS NEEDED

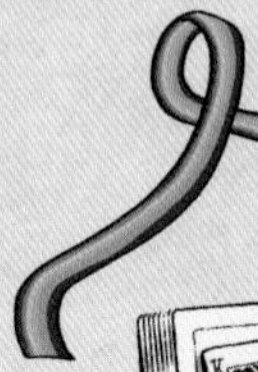

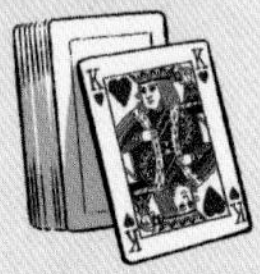

deck of cards

piece of colorful ribbon, at least 30 inches long

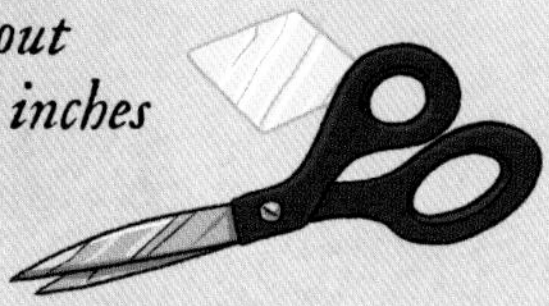

piece of thin, clear plastic, about 1½ square inches

scissors

PREPARATION

Use the scissors to cut a slot in the center of the square, large enough for the ribbon to slip through the slot smoothly.

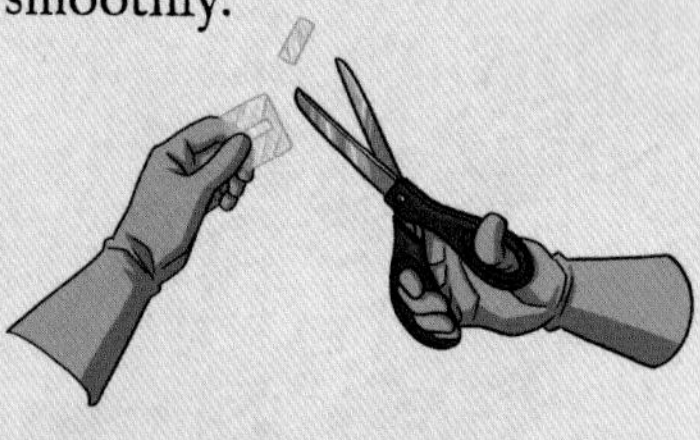

Thread the ribbon through the slot until about 4 to 5 inches of the ribbon are on one side of the plastic square.

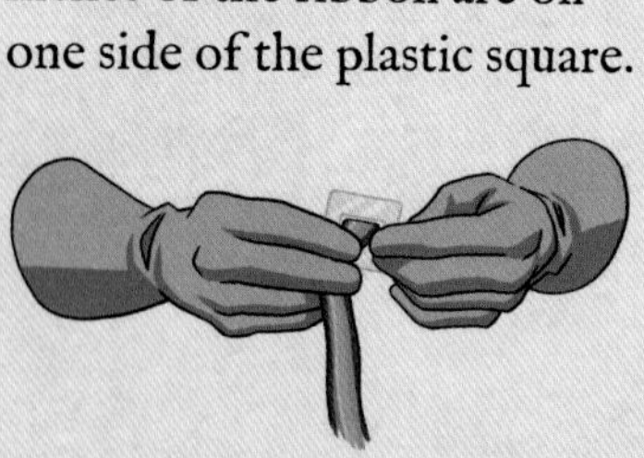

PERFORMANCE

1 While you liken the ribbon to the Bifrost and the deck of cards to Heimdall, place the plastic square with the ribbon on the front of the box of cards, at the center of the box. The long end of the ribbon will face the audience. It will cover the shorter end of the ribbon, which will also be pressed against the front of the box, with the short piece dangling just below the box.

2 Remind the audience that though the rainbow bridge can span every inch of the universe, transporting Asgardians to and from their home world, no one can gain entrance into the hallowed halls of the court of Odin without the approval of Heimdall. He, like the deck of cards, serves as the last and best protector of the realm.

Hold the box of cards so that your thumb is pressing the back of the box and your forefinger and middle finger are on either side of the ribbon, pressing the plastic square securely against the front of the box. With your free hand, grab the short end of the ribbon and hide it behind the box. The audience should only see the top ribbon.

3 Still pressing the plastic square against the box, tug on the end of the ribbon, reminding the audience that you are Loki—and no one, especially not a glorified hall monitor like Heimdall, can keep you from your mission.

As you pull, the ribbon will seem to be pulled out through the box. Keep pulling the ribbon completely through the plastic slot and "out" the back until you have reached the throne.

THE HEART OF IRON MAN

Tony Stark is a brilliant scientist, but he is also just a man. A man with many faults, not the least of which is his heart. Physically wounded and metaphorically in the hands of those he loves, his heart is protected by his super suit—but it can never be truly protected from your magic!

MATERIALS NEEDED

3 thin or lightweight scarves or handkerchiefs of the same size (preferably red, gold, and white)

fabric glue

clear drinking vessel

a length of black thread as long as the drinking vessel is high

rubber band

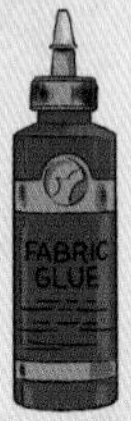
FABRIC
GLUE

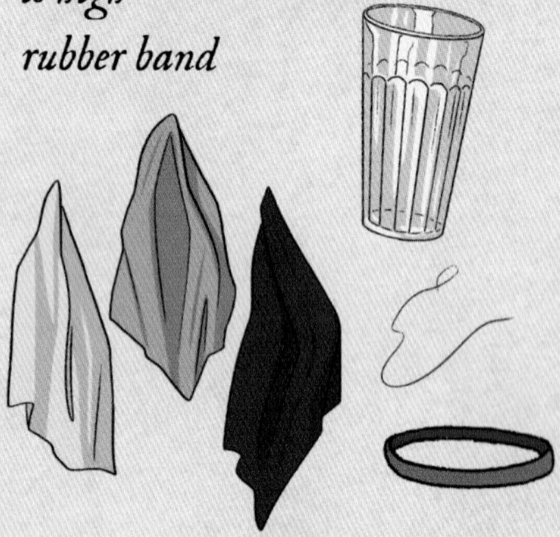

PREPARATION

Use the glue to attach one end of the black thread to a corner of the white scarf or handkerchief.

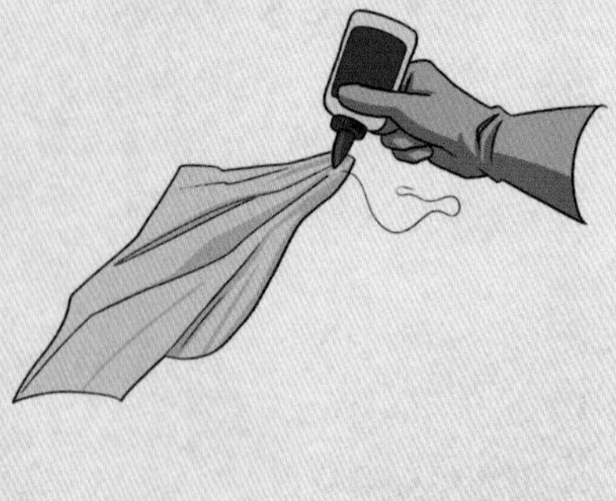

PERFORMANCE

1 Command that the audience take a moment to remember all the times Tony Stark has tried to defeat you. While they do, hold the clear drinking vessel in your left hand, and describe how much it is like his fragile and transparent ego. Tuck the white handkerchief inside of the glass, making sure the corner with thread glued to it is last to be pushed in and the thread is hanging out of the vessel. Place your left thumb on the thread, securing it to the side of the drinking vessel. Compare the color white to his too-human heart and the glow that emanates from the Unibeam Projector embedded in the chest of his Iron Man armor.

2 With the thread still secured against the vessel with your thumb, push the yellow handkerchief, representing the gold accents of his armor, inside the vessel and on top of the white one.

CONTINUED . . .

3 Lay the red handkerchief over the top of the vessel so it hides the entire vessel. Describe how it represents the remaining parts of his super suit.

Fasten the rubber band around the red handkerchief over the drinking glass, explaining to the audience that no matter how many layers of protection Tony Stark covers himself with, he will always be vulnerable to your magic.

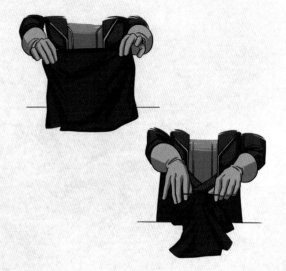

4 Holding the glass with one hand, reach under the red handkerchief with the other and pull on the black thread. Hidden by the red handkerchief, your tugging on the black thread will pull the white handkerchief past the gold handkerchief and over the lip of the vessel.

5 Tug directly on the white handkerchief once it is within reach. It will look as if it is being pulled through the bottom of the glass.

Toss the white handkerchief aside as you would a fallen Tony Stark. Remove the rubber band and the red handkerchief to reveal that the gold handkerchief is, as his useless armor would be, still there, protecting an empty void where the white handkerchief, and his heart, had been.

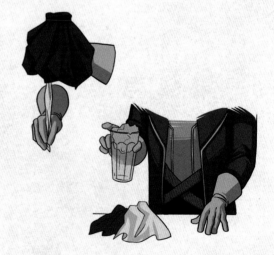

BROTHERS

As much as you have hated, hate, and will always hate to admit it, Thor is your brother. You both have certainly had disagreements, but you share a bond that no amount of magic can break. However much you try. This trick proves that you and Thor will always be a duo.

MATERIALS NEEDED

2 *Midgardian coins*

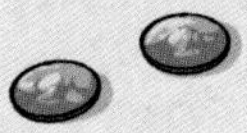

PREPARATION

Pick up a coin on the right side of the table with your left hand and toss it into your right hand until the toss and catch looks smooth and feels natural.

Practice pretending to toss the coin while actually keeping it in your left hand. When you toss, close your right hand as if you have caught the coin. However, turn your left wrist as you toss so the audience will not see you pinch the coin between your thumb and fingers and shift the coin into the palm of your left hand.

Practice picking up another coin on the table with your left hand, with the coin still held within your palm.

CONTINUED . . .

PERFORMANCE

1 Place two coins in front of you on the table, one for you and one for Thor.

2 Place the palm of your right hand down, over the right coin. Try to say something nice about Thor.

Place the palm of your right hand down, over the right coin. Try to narrow down all of the nice things you could say about yourself into one really good thing.

3 Turn your right hand over and place the back of your hand on the right coin.

Turn your left hand over and place the back of your left hand on the left coin.

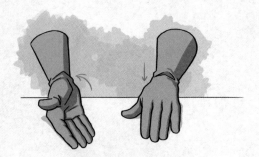

4 Pick up the coin on your right with your left hand and, as you pronounce Thor a fool, pretend to toss it to your right hand. Instead, keep the coin in your left hand.

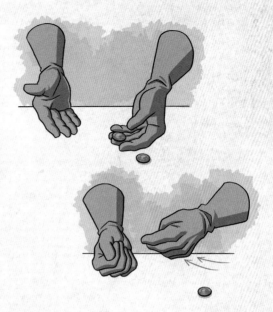

5 Place your right palm down as if you are placing a coin on the table.

Palm the coin in your left hand and place it down, over the other coin on the table.

With your right hand, rub the table where that coin "should" be.

6 Raise your right hand to reveal that the coin has vanished. Remind the audience that though Thor is a fool . . .

. . . he is your fool. Raise your left hand to reveal the two coins.

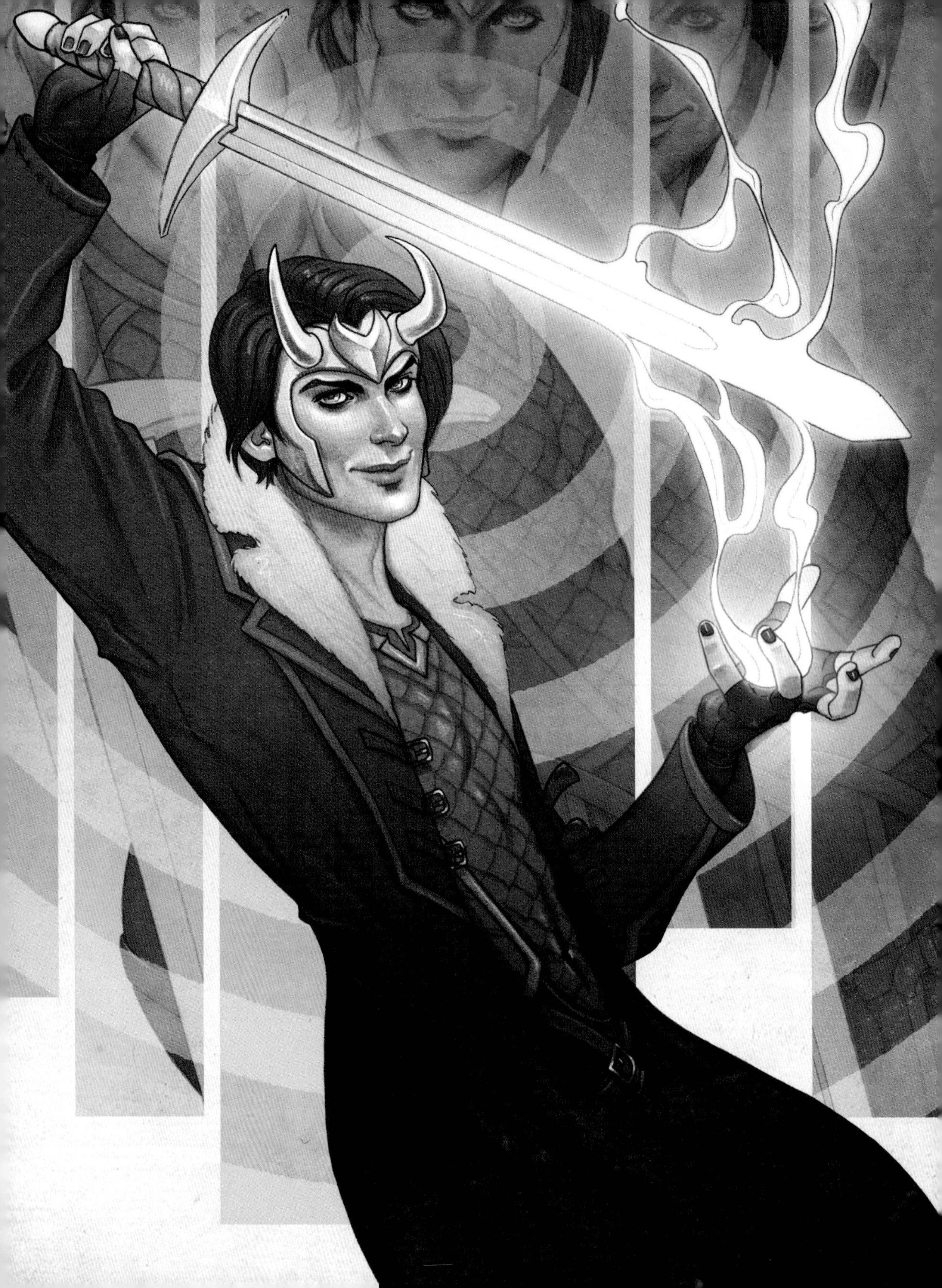

Dear Reader:

I've found one last trick in Loki's handwritten codex. If I'm reading it correctly (and I know I am), it is no less than instructions on how to travel to, and conquer, Asgard. It is called *A Triumphant Return*.

I have decided to follow Loki's instructions and traverse the realms myself. I trust I will be warmly welcomed by Odin and will take the original version of this book with me to donate to the Asgardian archives for history—and for safekeeping, should Loki ever try to reclaim it.

It is, by far, the most challenging spell of them all, requiring an array of materials spanning at least four—no, five—realms. I've tried eighty-five times already and fear I may be mistranslating one of the 1,962 words in the incantation. I'm frustrated but determined—no, obsessed—with the need to master this trick. I will try one more time and will transcribe the instructions and a specific list of materials needed to perform this feat when I've returned.

—RP

Publisher's Note: Though this book remains unfinished, we felt it should be published, both in the interest of the public and to honor Robb Pearlman's sacrifice.

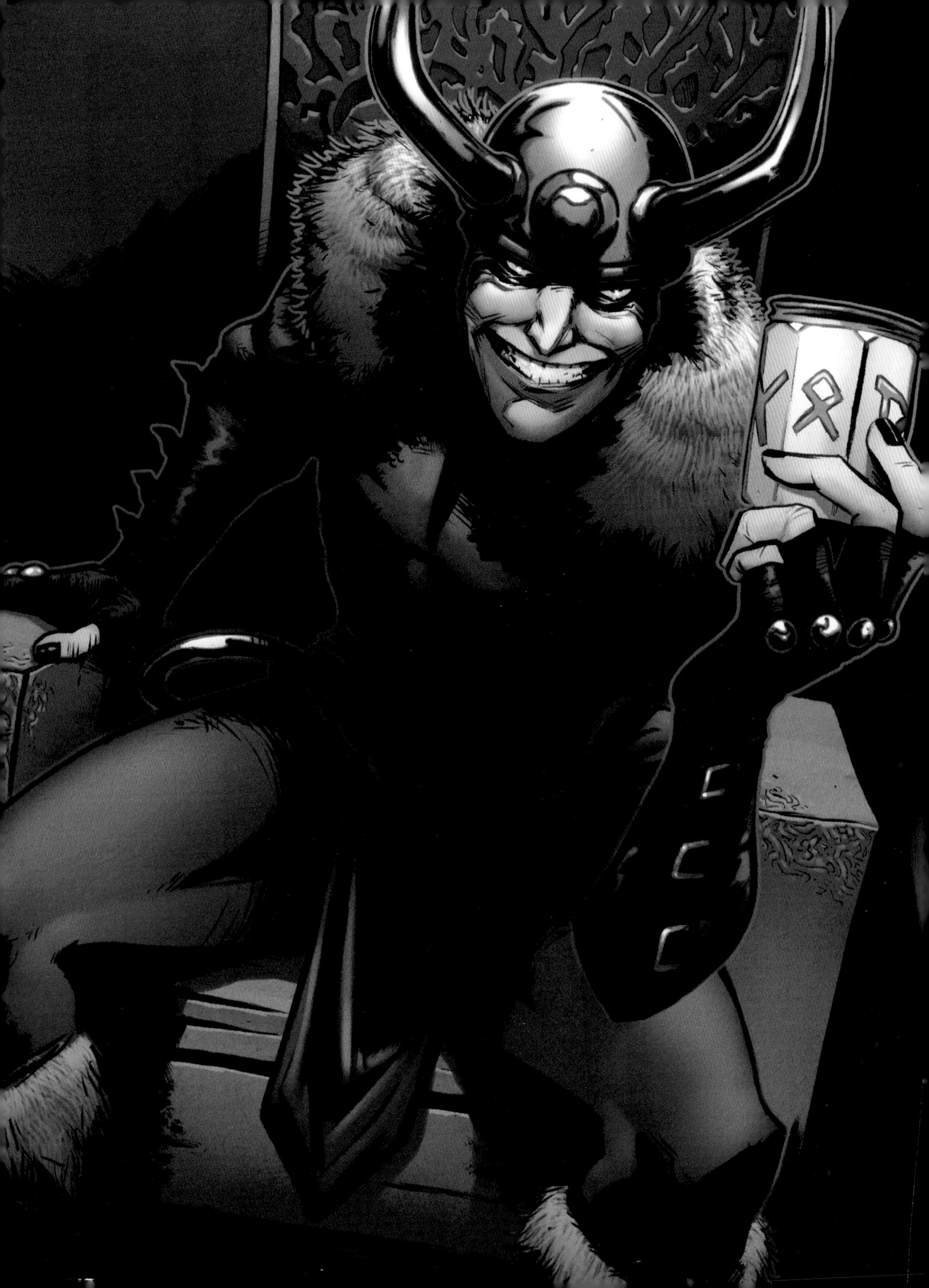